Afghanistan: U.S. Rule of Law and Justice Sector Assistance

Liana Sun Wyler
Analyst in International Crime and Narcotics

Kenneth Katzman
Specialist in Middle Eastern Affairs

November 9, 2010

Congressional Research Service

7-5700

www.crs.gov

R41484

Summary

Developing effective Afghan justice sector institutions is considered by many observers to be essential in winning the support of the Afghan population, improving the Afghan government's credibility and legitimacy, and reducing support for insurgent factions. Such sentiments are reinforced in the face of growing awareness of the pervasiveness of Afghan corruption. To this end, establishing the rule of law (ROL) in Afghanistan has become a priority in U.S. strategy for Afghanistan and an issue of interest to Congress. Numerous U.S. programs to promote ROL are in various stages of implementation and receive ongoing funding and oversight from Congress. Major programs include the following:

- State Department's Justice Sector Support Program (JSSP) and Corrections System Support Program (CSSP);

- U.S. Agency for International Development's (USAID's) formal and informal ROL stabilization programs (RLS);

- Justice Department's (DOJ's) Senior Federal Prosecutors Program, which, with State Department funds, provides legal mentoring and training; and

- Defense Department's (DOD's) operational support through Combined Joint Task Force 101 (CJTF-101), as well as through Combined Joint Interagency Task Force 435 (CJIATF-435).

It is difficult to identify all the programs, activities, and actors involved in ROL in Afghanistan, in part because of the continued evolution of U.S. strategy and interagency coordination for supporting the Afghan justice sector. Among the most recent shifts in strategy, U.S. efforts are increasingly resourced by a surge in civilian personnel at the provincial and district levels. To align with counterinsurgency (COIN) objectives, the U.S. government is emphasizing not only ministerial-level institution-building, but also projects to improve local-level access to justice, including projects to support informal dispute resolution mechanisms. Policy coordination among U.S. civilian and military entities involved in ROL efforts in Afghanistan also continues to change—including, most recently, the establishment of an Ambassador-led Coordinating Director for Rule of Law and Law Enforcement (CDROLLE) directorate at the U.S. Embassy, a General-led Rule of Law Field Force (ROLFF) under the CJIATF-435, as well as an Interagency Planning and Implementation Team (IPIT) to coordinate all civilian and military ROL activities in Afghanistan. Future shifts in policy approaches may also occur as policymakers seek to address growing concerns regarding Afghan corruption.

Observers debate whether or to what extent the increased U.S. commitment to and resources for ROL efforts in Afghanistan will help the U.S. government reach its ultimate goal of developing a stable, capable, and legitimate Afghan government. Many would argue that the challenges in Afghanistan to ROL development and justice sector reform remain substantial and many factors undermine prospects for success. Chief among these are ongoing allegations of severe corruption at all levels of the Afghan government, lack of overall security and stability, limited Afghan government capacity, the existence of competing justice mechanisms, and the persistence of traditional attitudes that perpetuate the perception that well-connected Afghans can avoid facing prosecution and conviction. These debates will likely continue in the 112th Congress, as Members remain concerned with all aspects of U.S. policy toward Afghanistan, including authorizing and appropriating ROL-related programs and assistance, as well as conducting oversight on policy implementation and effectiveness.

Contents

Figures

Tables

Contacts

Purpose and Scope

The purpose of this report is to provide background and analysis for Congress on U.S. rule of law (ROL) and justice sector assistance programs to Afghanistan. This report provides context for ROL issues in Afghanistan by defining ROL and the justice sector, describing the scope of the ROL problem in Afghanistan, including the role of corruption, and surveying the range of Afghan justice sector institutions. This report also describes U.S., Afghan, and multilateral policy approaches to the Afghan justice sector since the U.S. military invasion of Afghanistan in 2001, U.S. policy coordination and funding, and current U.S. justice sector assistance programs in Afghanistan.

Additionally, this report examines several issues for the 112th Congress, which is likely to remain concerned with all aspects of U.S. policy toward Afghanistan, including authorizing and appropriating ROL-related programs and assistance, as well as oversight on policy implementation and effectiveness. Issues for Congress include the implications of Afghan corruption on future U.S. foreign assistance to Afghanistan, limitations of U.S. ROL support efforts in Afghanistan, debates regarding U.S. support to the Afghan informal justice sector, and long-term effectiveness of U.S. ROL support efforts in Afghanistan. U.S. efforts to train and support Afghan police forces as well as counternarcotics and anti-corruption efforts are discussed due to their cross-cutting relationship to ROL, but they are not the primary focus of this report.

Background

After several decades of conflict, warlordism, and government misrule, the U.S. government and international community began to rebuild the Afghan government's capacity, including ROL institutions, following the 2001 fall of the Taliban.[1] Helping Afghanistan build its justice sector, however, suffers from the same difficulties that have complicated all efforts to expand and reform governance in that country: lack of trained human capital; traditional affiliation patterns that undermine the professionalism, neutrality, and impartiality of official institutions; and complications from the broader lack of security and stability in Afghanistan.

At stake in U.S. government and multilateral efforts to support ROL development in Afghanistan is the goal of a stable, capable, and legitimate Afghan government. In a report evaluating ROL programs in Afghanistan, the State Department's Inspector General's Office (OIG) states:

> In Afghanistan, there is a direct connect between the lack of a workable system of governance and the national security of the United States. The absence of a modern, functional government sustains the Taliban and Al Qaeda and encourages the rapid growth of the opium trade. Confidence that the government can provide a fair and effective justice system is an important element in convincing war-battered Afghans to build their future in a democratic system rather than reverting to one dominated by terrorists, warlords, and

---

[1] In that year, the U.S. government decided to militarily overthrow the Taliban when it refused to extradite Osama bin Laden after the September 11, 2001, attacks, judging that a friendly regime in Kabul was needed to enable U.S forces to search for Al Qaeda activists there. For more, see CRS Report RL30588, *Afghanistan: Post-Taliban Governance, Security, and U.S. Policy*, by Kenneth Katzman.

narcotics traffickers. Without ROL the country cannot progress no matter what contributions are made by outsiders.[2]

By all accounts, the challenges in Afghanistan confronting ROL development and justice sector reform remain substantial. Limits to ROL reflect deficiencies in or the absence of effective national laws, police forces, and judicial systems. Afghanistan suffers from significant resource limitations in implementing a formal ROL system and from high levels of corruption. By most accounts, official corruption, which involves the misuse of public office for private gain, permeates all sectors of governance and is particularly prevalent in the law enforcement and judicial sectors. The legitimacy of Afghan national law continues to be challenged by alternate power structures, including tribal and militia leaders, and the Taliban, as well as major faction or ethnic leaders.[3] U.S. and Afghan officials have raised concerns that, in the absence of effective ROL and a functioning formal justice system, Afghans may turn to or be forced to use the Taliban justice system to resolve disputes.[4]

Scope of the ROL Problem in Afghanistan

A multiplicity of factors work against establishing ROL in Afghanistan. These factors include:

Lack of Overall Security and Stability. It is difficult to establish ROL—and governance in general—throughout Afghanistan, but particularly in areas where consistent combat is occurring. Out of the 364 districts of Afghanistan, the Defense Department (DOD) has identified 120 of them as either "Key Terrain" or "Area of Interest" districts, meaning that the United States and its partners are devoting substantial resources to the securing and stabilization of those districts.

Negative Perceptions of the Afghan Government. It is widely reported that many Afghans perceive their government as corrupt and "predatory," and that perception complicates efforts by the international community and Afghan government to instill public trust in Afghanistan's justice sector institutions.

Limited Capacity of the Afghan Government. Virtually all Afghans, including those that have confidence in the Afghan government, complain that it lacks capacity. Only about 30% of the adult population is literate, meaning that, even in secure areas, it is difficult to recruit sufficient numbers of Afghans to serve in justice sector institutions. Recruiting public servants also is made difficult by the push-pull effect of low wages offered for government service and higher wages offered by international donor organizations. According to reports, approximately 60% of Afghan civil servants are over the age of 50, suggesting that younger Afghans are not choosing public service careers.

Existence of Competing Justice Mechanisms. Some Afghans are skeptical of Western or modern models of justice, and find traditional justice mechanisms easier to access and to understand. Some of these mechanisms are practiced in areas under insurgent control, although only 2% of those who preferred to resolve disputes through non-state justice providers resorted to Taliban courts, according to some outside estimates.

Traditional Attitudes. Efforts to build ROL in Afghanistan are also hampered by traditional attitudes and affiliations. A common perception, based on key examples, is that well connected Afghans—defined as personal, ethnic, and factional ties to those who run the justice sector—can avoid facing prosecution or conviction.

Source: Congressional Research Service.

---

[2] U.S. Department of State and Broadcasting Board of Governors, Office of the Inspector General (OIG), "Rule-of-Law Programs in Afghanistan," Report No. ISP-I-08-09, January 2008, p. 1. See also Gretchen Peters, Crime and Insurgency in the Tribal Areas of Afghanistan and Pakistan, Harmony Project, Combating Terrorism Center, October 15, 2010.

[3] U.S. Department of Defense (DOD), the Judge Advocate General's Legal Center and School, U.S. Army and the Center for Law and Military Operations, *Rule of Law Handbook: A Practitioner's Guide for Judge Advocates*, 2009, 3rd ed., p. 235.

[4] See for example Nader Nadery, a commissioner in the Afghan Independent Human Rights Commission, "Peace Needs to Get Serious About Justice," *Parliamentary Brief*, September 2010.

Given the challenges facing ROL efforts and the perceived security imperative to address current ROL shortcomings in Afghanistan, ROL efforts have become the subject of increasing attention within the Obama Administration's strategy for achieving U.S. goals in Afghanistan.[5] Several U.S. policy and guidance documents provide a framework for U.S. participation in ROL operations in Afghanistan, including the 2009 *Integrated Civilian-Military Campaign Plan* and the 2010 *Afghanistan and Pakistan Regional Stabilization Strategy*, both of which identify as top priorities the strengthening of Afghan ROL and access to justice.[6] While not formally approved, the U.S. government has also maintained draft strategies that specifically address ROL efforts and, separately, anti-corruption efforts in Afghanistan.[7]

Defining ROL

In 2004, the United Nations (UN) Secretary-General described ROL as a "principle of governance" characterized by adherence to the principles of supremacy of law, equality before the law, accountability to the law, fairness in the application of the law, separation of powers, participation in decision-making, legal certainty, avoidance of arbitrariness, and procedural and legal transparency.[8] Under this concept, "all persons, institutions and entities, public and private... are accountable to laws" publicly promulgated, equally enforced, independently adjudicated, and consistent with international human rights law. This definition is widely applied, including in official U.S. government documents by the Departments of State and Defense.

ROL is often understood to be a foundational element for the establishment and maintenance of democracy and economic growth, and the vehicle through which fundamental political, social, and economic rights are protected and enforced. The concept assumes the existence of effective and legitimate institutions, primarily a country's national government, to administer the law as well as to guarantee personal security and public order. ROL also requires citizen confidence in

---

[5] See The White House, Office of the Press Secretary, President Barack Obama, "Remarks by the President on a New Strategy for Afghanistan and Pakistan," March 27, 2009, available at http://www.whitehouse.gov/the_press_office/ Remarks-by-the-President-on-a-New-Strategy-for-Afghanistan-and-Pakistan.

[6] Several additional overarching U.S. government strategies, whose primary focus are not rule of law (ROL) and not specifically directed toward Afghanistan, nevertheless touch on the subject. These include the National Security Presidential Directive 44 (NSPD-44), issued by President George W. Bush on December 7, 2005; DOD Decision Directive 3000.05; and the U.S. Army Counterinsurgency Field Manual 3-24 (FM-3-24). NSPD-44 establishes that the Department of State is responsible for planning and implementing U.S. reconstruction and development assistance, which includes ROL. DOD Directive 3000.05, issued on November 28, 2005, establishes stability operations as a "core U.S. military mission" and identifies the "long-term goal" of such missions as helping to "develop indigenous capacity for securing essential services, a viable market economy, rule of law, democratic institutions, and a robust civil society." FM 3-24, revised in December 2006, states that "establishing the rule of law is a key goal and end state in COIN." ROL is described as including support to host nation police, legal code, judicial courts, and penal system.

[7] U.S. Department of State, U.S. Embassy Kabul, response to CRS request, April 21, 2009. The creation of such a strategy was first mandated by the National Security Council in 2008 and is intended to coordinate all elements of U.S. government ROL activities, civilian and military.

[8] United Nations, Report of the Secretary-General, "The Rule of Law and Transitional Justice in Conflict and Post-Conflict Societies," S/2004/616, August 23, 2004, p. 4. Other definitions for ROL also exist. For example, the State Department's OIG described ROL, in the context of an inspection report of Embassy Baghdad, Iraq, as "the entire legal complex of a modern state—from a constitution and a legislature to courts, judges, police, prisons, due process procedures, a commercial code and anticorruption measures." However, this 2004 U.N. definition has become a standard in the justice sector community, referenced, among others, by the State Department and Defense Department in official documents. For the OIG report on Embassy Baghdad, see U.S. Department of State and the Broadcasting Board of Governors, OIG, "Inspection of Rule-of-Law Programs, Embassy Baghdad," Report No. ISP-IQO-06-01, October 2005.

the fairness and effectiveness of its application, including procedural fairness, protection of human rights and civil liberties, and access to justice. The absence of significant government corruption is considered a prerequisite for effective ROL to be established, because only in corruption's absence is the supremacy of law upheld.

While ROL is dependent on all aspects of governance to function properly, it is the "justice sector" that is responsible for ensuring that the ROL is implemented.[9] The justice sector thus encompasses the entire legal apparatus of a country and its society, including the criminal as well as the civil and commercial justice sectors. Administration of justice can take place through formal, state-run judicial mechanisms as well as through traditional, or informal, dispute resolution mechanisms. In additional to the formal judiciary, additional elements of the justice sector are drawn from the executive and legislative branches, as well as other public and private institutions. They include the ministries of justice, legislatures, law enforcement agencies, prisons, financial and commercial regulatory bodies, prosecutors' offices, public defenders, ombudsmen's offices, law schools, bar associations, legal assistance, non-governmental organizations (NGOs), legal advocacy organizations, and customary and religious non-state dispute resolution institutions.[10]

ROL plays a prominent role in counterinsurgency (COIN) operations and can take place in post-conflict situations as well. As part of such efforts, a common objective of ROL efforts is to help establish or strengthen a legitimate governing authority and framework to which the local populace gives consent. According to the revised 2006 U.S. Army COIN field manual, establishing the ROL is a "key goal and end state."[11] Civilian planning efforts for post-conflict situations similarly include ROL as a component of their missions. The U.S. Department of State's Office of the Coordinator for Reconstruction and Stabilization (S/CRS) lists "justice and reconciliation" as one of five key components to post-conflict reconstruction "essential tasks"; under this heading, justice and reconciliation includes capacity building elements associated with the criminal justice system, indigenous police, judicial personnel and infrastructure, legal system reform, corrections, and human rights, among others.[12]

In post-conflict situations, a prerequisite for the establishment of permanent, democratic ROL may be the implementation first of "transitional justice." According to the United Nations, transitional justice comprises the "full range of processes and mechanisms associated with a society's attempt to come to terms with a legacy of large-scale past abuses, in order to ensure accountability, serve justice, and achieve reconciliation." Transitional justice may include both judicial and non-judicial activities that may variously include individual prosecutions, reparations, truth-seeking, institutional reform, and vetting and dismissals. Transitional justice may also include efforts to rebuild justice sector institutions that were destroyed or lack the capacity to fulfill its basic functions and responsibilities.

---

[9] Justice, as conceived by the United Nations, is viewed as a universal concept that can be found among all national cultures and traditions. The United Nations defines "justice" as an "ideal of accountability and fairness in the protection and vindication of rights and the prevention and punishment of wrongs." United Nations, Report of the Secretary-General, "The Rule of Law and Transitional Justice in Conflict and Post-Conflict Societies," S/2004/616, August 23, 2004, p. 4.

[10] See U.S. Agency for International Development (USAID), Office of Democracy and Governance, Rule of Law Division, "Guide to Rule of Law Country Analysis: The Rule of Law Strategic Framework," August 2008, pp. 13-16.

[11] U.S. Army Counterinsurgency Field Manual 3-24 (FM-3-24).

[12] See U.S. Department of State, Office of the Coordinator for Reconstruction and Stabilization (S/CRS), *Post-Conflict Reconstruction Essential Tasks*, April 2005; Fm 3-24, pp. D-8 and D-9.

Transitional justice mechanisms and efforts to rebuild or strengthen justice sector institutions in post-conflict situations can be undermined by spoilers and opposition forces.[13] Particularly in post-conflict situations, powerful leaders and political figures that had previously benefitted from the absence of ROL may attempt to resist efforts that could result in the reduction of their political influence, social status, and financial interests. They can include formal opposition groups, such as political parties, NGOs, and religious groups. They can also include informal or illicit opposition groups, such as insurgents, local militias, warlords, "for-hire" armed groups, and organized crime and corruption networks.

For Afghanistan, the term ROL has been used in the contexts described above. Justice sector assistance programs in Afghanistan have historically centered on efforts to build the capacity of the formal justice institutions (e.g., Supreme Court, Ministry of Justice, and Attorney General's Office). While current police and counternarcotics efforts in Afghanistan have ROL components, these programs have historically been implemented and evaluated separately from other ROL programs. Support to the Afghan National Police (ANP), for example, is mainly funded and categorized as a component of support to the security forces and security sector. Since the early 2000s, when the first formal U.S. government ROL programs were developed in Afghanistan, ROL programs have evolved to include greater emphasis on dispute resolution mechanisms that comprise the informal justice sector. This development is both considered central to the counterinsurgency (COIN) strategy in Afghanistan and controversial among human rights advocates.

Perceptions of Corruption in Afghanistan

Corruption, involving the abuse of power, trust, or position for private or personal gain, can have widespread negative effects on the establishment of ROL, democratic governance, and economic development.[14] It can undermine efforts to establish democracy by threatening the viability of publicly accountable and transparent government institutions. It can also exacerbate inequality in a society when there is a perception that government services and foreign donor aid funds are only available through bribery or extortion to those who can pay the highest price. Political interference in the justice sector in particular can compromise the impartiality and integrity of judicial processes by fostering a culture of impunity.

The presence of such widespread and entrenched corruption in Afghanistan is widely assessed to be undermining Afghan public and international donor confidence in the ability to establish ROL in Afghanistan.[15] Despite differences in methodology and scope, studies agree that corruption in Afghanistan is a significant and growing problem. According to a 2009 U.S. Agency for International Development (USAID) assessment, the country is challenged by "pervasive, entrenched, and systemic corruption" that has reached unprecedented levels (see **Figure 1**).[16] Such corruption is reportedly undermining security, development, and state-building objectives.

---

[13] DOD, *Rule of Law Handbook*, 3rd ed., p. 218.

[14] See for example Transparency International, *Global Corruption Report*, 2004, 2005, and 2009.

[15] A more extensive discussion of the sources and types of corruption in Afghanistan is contained in: CRS Report RS21922, *Afghanistan: Politics, Elections, and Government Performance*, by Kenneth Katzman.

[16] USAID, "Assessment of Corruption in Afghanistan," January 15, 2009, through March 1, 2009, written under contract by Checchi and Company Consulting, Inc., Report No. PNADO248.

According to the NGO Transparency International, Afghanistan in 2009 was ranked the second-most corrupt country in the world (179 out of 180 countries ranked).

Figure 1. Population Survey Results on Afghan Government Challenges

Responses to the Question "What is the Biggest Problem that the Government has to Address?"

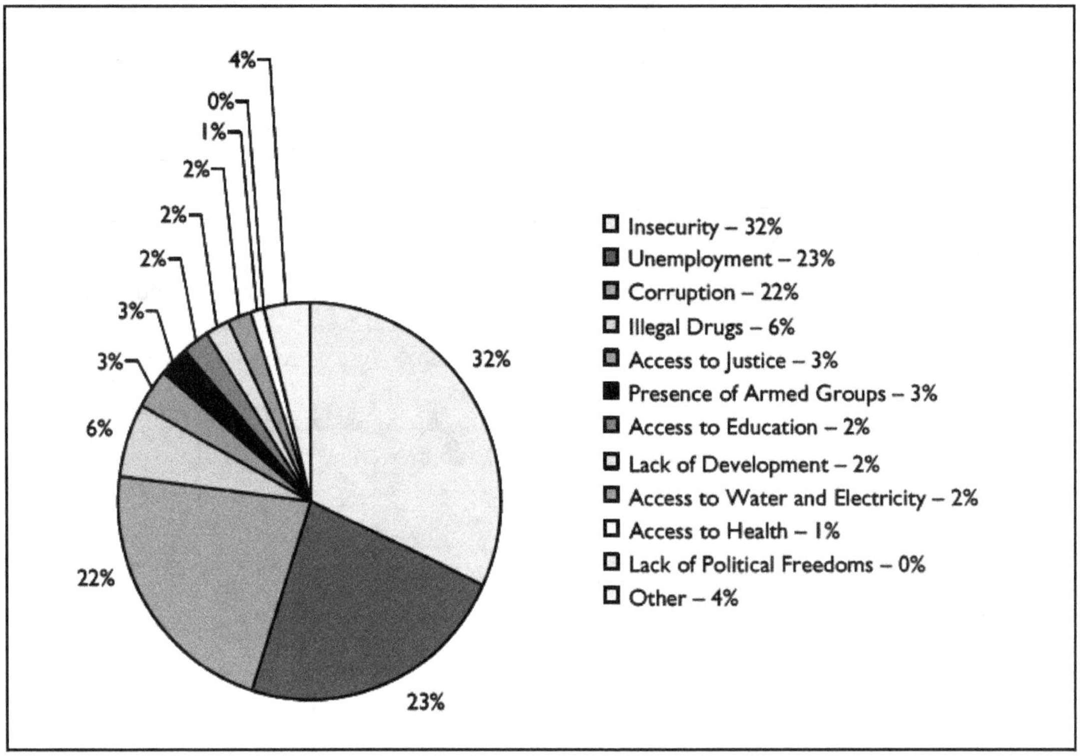

Source: CRS graphic of data from Integrity Watch Afghanistan, "Afghan Perceptions and Experiences of Corruption: A National Survey 2010," 2010, p. 26.

Note: Other recent Afghan population surveys found similar overall trends in terms of the top problems facing Afghanistan today and in terms of the particular problem of corruption. For example, the United Nations Office on Drugs and Crime (UNODC) found that 59% of Afghans surveyed identified corruption as the biggest problem in Afghanistan. Similarly, the Asia Foundation found that 76% of respondents agreed that corruption is a major problem for Afghanistan.

At the upper levels of government, several press accounts and observers have asserted that Afghan President Hamid Karzai deliberately tolerates officials who are allegedly involved in the narcotics trade and other illicit activity. Press accounts further assert that President Karzai supports such officials' receipt of lucrative contracts from donor countries, in exchange for their political support. Examples of cronyism and favoritism were evident in early September 2010, when President Karzai ousted the management of the large Kabul Bank, which processes payments for public sector employees, because of revelations of excessively large loans to major shareholders. Among them are Mahmoud Karzai, the President's elder brother, who is a major shareholder of Kabul Bank, and the brother of First Vice President Muhammad Fahim.[17]

---

[17] Dexter Filkins, "Run on Deposits Fuels Bank Crisis in Afghanistan," *New York Times*, September 3, 2010.

Aside from the issue of high level nepotism, observers say that most of the governmental corruption takes place in the course of performing mundane governmental functions, such as government processing of official documents (e.g., passports, drivers' licenses), in which those who process these documents routinely demand bribes in exchange for more rapid action.[18] Other forms of corruption include Afghan security officials' selling U.S. and internationally provided vehicles, fuel, and equipment to supplement their salaries. In other cases, local police or border officials may siphon off customs revenues or demand extra payments to help guard the U.S. or other militaries' equipment shipments. Other examples include cases in which security commanders have placed "no show" persons on official payrolls in order to pocket their salaries. At a broader level, the U.S. Special Inspector General for Afghanistan Reconstruction (SIGAR) has assessed that the mandate of Afghanistan's Control and Audit Office (CAO) is too narrow and lacks the independence needed to serve as an effective watch over the use of Afghan government funds.[19]

Population survey-based assessments appear to support the view that it is the lower level corruption that most affects the population and colors its assessment of government. Government corruption registers as among the top problems facing Afghanistan today.[20] The majority of respondents also identify corruption as having become a more significant problem compared to the prior year and as having consistently increased in scope and severity since 2006.[21] According to the United Nations Office on Drugs and Crime (UNODC), as many as one out of every two Afghans experienced bribery in the past year, resulting in an estimated $2.5 billion in bribe payments in 2009 alone—an amount that almost rivals the estimated value of the Afghan drug trade.[22] The average value of a single administrative bribe in Afghanistan in 2009, according to the cited studies, was reportedly between $156 and $160 and, among those who paid bribes, the average number of bribes paid per year was reportedly between 3.4 times and five times per year.

Afghanistan's Justice Sector Institutions

Afghan institutions engaged in the justice sector comprise a mix of formal governing institutions and offices, as mandated by the 2004 Afghan Constitution, as well as a broad range of informal dispute resolution mechanisms. A centerpiece of early U.S. government and international ROL efforts was the development and final Afghan approval of a new Constitution, which formally created a central government, a bi-cameral legislature, and an independent judiciary. Elements of Afghanistan's legal infrastructure included judges, prosecutors, courthouses, prisons, and secular and *Sharia* faculties of law.

---

[18] Dexter Filkins, "Bribes Corrode Afghan's Trust in Government," *New York Times*, January 2, 2009.

[19] Aamer Madhani, "U.S. Reviews Afghan Watchdog Authority." *USA Today*, May 12, 2010.

[20] The Asia Foundation, "Afghanistan in 2009: A Survey of the Afghan People," 2009, p. 69; United Nations Office on Drugs and Crime (UNODC), "Corruption in Afghanistan: Bribery as Reported by the Victims," January 2010, p.3; Integrity Watch Afghanistan, "Afghan Perceptions and Experiences of Corruption: A National Survey 2010," 2010, p. 26.

[21] Integrity Watch Afghanistan, p. 23. According to the Integrity Watch survey, 75% of respondents said corruption has become more significant. The Asia Foundation, "Afghanistan in 2009: A Survey of the Afghan People," 2009, pp. 70-71. According to the Asia Foundation survey, the proportion of respondents who identify corruption as a major problem in their daily life and in their neighborhood has been rising steadily since 2006.

[22] UNODC, "Corruption in Afghanistan: Bribery as Reported by the Victims," January 2010, p. 4. Note that another survey found a much lower, but nevertheless significant, estimate. According to Integrity Watch Afghanistan, one in seven adults experienced direct bribery in 2009. Integrity Watch Afghanistan, p. 10.

Due in part to the limited reach of the formal justice system to many parts of the country, as well as ongoing general distrust and lack of familiarity with the formal justice system, many Afghans have continued to rely on traditional, local forms of dispute resolution, which are generally characterized as informal justice systems (see **Figure 2**). Such traditional bodies are believed to vary significantly among the 364 districts that comprise Afghanistan and the degree to which they provide just, fair, and humane resolutions to disputes remains a source of debate among observers.

Figure 2. Population Survey Results on Perceptions of the Formal and Informal Justice Sector

Proportion of Respondents Who Agree With the Five Following Statements on the Formal (State Courts) and Informal Justice Sectors (Local Jirga, Shura)

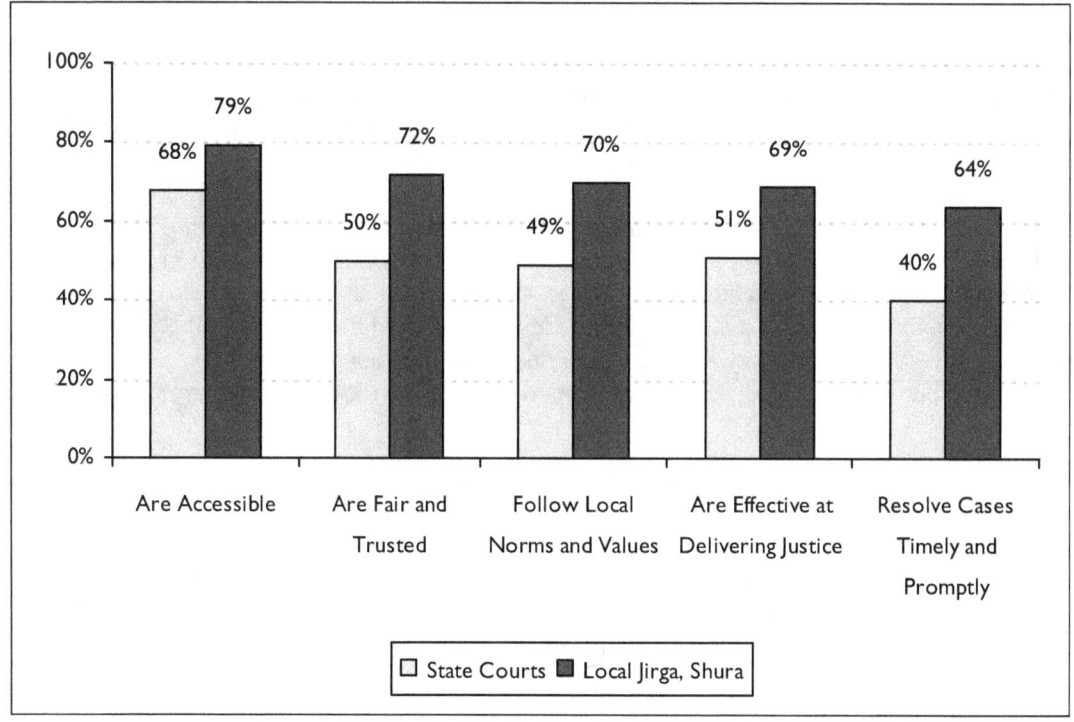

Source: CRS graphic of The Asia Foundation, "Afghanistan in 2009: A Survey of the Afghan People," 2009, p. 87 and p. 91.

The following sections describe, in turn, the various components of the formal and informal justice sectors. Included is a discussion of several of the key anti-corruption bodies within the formal Afghan justice system, which have been at the heart of recent controversy and policy discussion both in Afghanistan and the United States.

Quick Guide to Afghan Justice Sector Institutions

INDEPENDENT JUDICIARY

The Judiciary branch is composed of one Supreme Court, Courts of Appeals, and primary courts that are regulated and organized by law. Under the Supreme Court's jurisdiction are two specialized entities, which are in part U.S.-funded: (1) the Counter Narcotics Tribunal and (CNT) (2) the Anti-Corruption Tribunal (ACT).

EXECUTIVE BRANCH

Office of the Attorney General: The Attorney General's Office (AGO) investigates and prosecutes crimes, including cases of official corruption. Located within the AGO is a vetted and U.S.-supported Anti-Corruption Unit (ACU).

Ministry of Justice: The Ministry of Justice (MOJ) drafts, reviews, and vets proposed laws for compliance with the Constitution. It is also tasked with administering Afghanistan's prison system, including the Central Prisons Directorate (CPD).

Ministry of Interior: The Ministry of Interior (MOI) is responsible for overseeing domestic security, including the Afghan National Police (ANP). The Counter Narcotics Police (CNP), a subset of the ANP, oversee the Sensitive Investigative Unit (SIU).

High Office of Oversight: Established in 2008, the High Office of Oversight (HOO) identifies and refers corruption cases to prosecutors. The HOO also has the power to catalogue the overseas assets of Afghan officials.

Major Crimes Task Force: The Major Crimes Task Force (MCTF) is an interagency (and internationally funded) entity established in late 2009. It is tasked with investigating high-level public corruption, organized crime, and kidnapping cases.

INFORMAL DISPUTE RESOLUTION MECHANISMS

Local Shuras and Jirgas: Local informal dispute resolution mechanisms are run by *mullahs*, *mawlawis*, or other local elders and religious figures. In some Taliban-controlled areas of Afghanistan, the Taliban run local dispute resolution mechanisms.

Source: Congressional Research Service.

Formal Justice Sector Institutions

Under the Afghan Constitution, approved in a "Constitutional Loya Jirga" in January 2004, Afghanistan's central government has several major law enforcement institutions, which are discussed in the following sections.

Supreme Court

Chapter seven of Afghanistan's Constitution spells out the role of the Judicial branch of its government. The judicial branch consists of one Supreme Court, Courts of Appeals, and primary courts that are regulated and organized by law. The Supreme Court is the highest judicial organ. The nine members of the Supreme Court are appointed by the President to ten year terms, subject to their confirmation by the elected lower house of parliament (*Wolesi Jirga*, House of the People). The Supreme Court's primary role is to ensure that laws, decrees, treaties, and conventions comport with the provisions of the Constitution. The Supreme Court's budget also funds the work of the whole judicial branch of government, and the Court recommends appointments of judges throughout the judicial branch, subject to the concurrence of the President.

The head of the Supreme Court is Abdul Salam Azimi. He became Chief Justice of the Supreme Court in 2006, after the lower house of parliament refused to re-confirm his hardline Islamist

---

predecessor Fazl Hadi Shinwari. Azimi is a U.S. educated former university professor, and considered a reformer and a progressive. Formerly a legal advisor to Afghan President Hamid Karzai, Azimi played a key role in the drafting of the 2004 Constitution. However, some well-placed Afghan observers say that Azimi is not viewed as a key official in government and his influence is highly limited.[23]

Office of the Attorney General

According to article seven of the Constitution, the Attorney General is an independent office of the executive branch. Its duties are to investigate and prosecute crimes. It is the Attorney General's Office (AGO) that is tasked with prosecuting cases of official corruption. As part of the effort to expand ROL in Afghanistan, international donors are funding the construction of AGO provincial headquarters in each of Afghanistan's 34 provinces.

The Attorney General is Mohammad Ishaq Aloko. He was appointed Attorney General in August 2008, after Karzai fired his predecessor purportedly for expressing interest in running against Karzai in the August 2009 presidential election. Aloko was an intelligence officer for the government of Mohammad Daoud, who ruled Afghanistan from 1973 to 1978, and Aloko took refuge in Germany when Communist governments took power in 1978. He is a Pashtun, from Qandahar, which is the political base of Karzai.

A controversy erupted in August 2010 when Karzai ordered Deputy Attorney General Fazel Ahmad Faqriyar, to step down ostensibly for reaching the maximum 40 years of government service. However, calling into question independence of the office, Faqriyar said he was fired for refusing to block corruption investigations of high level officials, including four ministers.[24]

Ministry of Justice

The Ministry of Justice (MOJ) has primary responsibilities for judicial affairs of the executive branch. Its main duty is to draft, review, or vet proposed laws for compliance with Afghanistan's Constitution. It also has responsibility for administering Afghanistan's prison system. That authority was transferred to the MOJ from the Ministry of Interior (MOI) in 2003, in part because most Afghans identify the MOI with torture and abuses during the Soviet occupation period. The Justice Minister, appointed and confirmed by the National Assembly in January 2010, is Habibullah Ghaleb. He is a Tajik who worked in the Ministry during the reign of King Zahir Shah and his successor, and then as deputy Attorney General during the 1992-1996 *mujahedin*-led government of Burhanuddin Rabbani. He was part of Afghanistan's delegation to the July 2007 Rome Conference on rebuilding Afghanistan's justice sector.

Ministry of Interior

The Ministry of Interior (MOI) is responsible for overseeing domestic security organs. Today, the MOI is primarily focused on combating the insurgency rather than preventing crime. The Ministry manages the Afghan National Police (ANP), which now numbers about 110,000, and is trained by the United States and partner forces in Afghanistan. The Ministry has struggled to curb

---

[23] CRS conversations with former Karzai National Security Council aide. October 2010.

[24] Deb Reichman, "Corruption Probe Ruffles US-Afghan Relations," *Associated Press*, August 31, 2010.

the widely alleged corruption within the police forces, which has eroded the trust of the population in the ANP. Another factor that has contributed to lack of trust is the memory some Afghans have of the Ministry's role in suppressing domestic opposition to the Soviet occupation of Afghanistan, and the alleged torture conducted against captured *mujahedin* and other rebels in Afghanistan's prisons.

The current Interior Minister, Bismillah Khan, assumed his position in July 2010, after his predecessor, Mohammad Hanif Atmar, was dismissed suddenly in June 2010 over disagreements with President Karzai. Atmar reportedly disagreed with Karzai over the terms on which to potentially reconcile with Taliban insurgent leaders and on other issues. Khan, a Tajik, was the highly regarded Chief of Staff of the Afghan National Army (ANA) and his appointment to Interior Minister was intended, partly, to restore ethnic balance in the security apparatus. Most of the top leadership of the security organs is Pashtun.

Anti-corruption and Oversight Bodies

The following section describes major anti-corruption and oversight entities in Afghanistan and recent developments regarding their status. In 2010, heightened international concern over the level and extent of Afghan corruption, as well as ongoing challenges to Afghan governance overall, have increased scrutiny of several of these agencies. In particular, reports indicate that President Karzai has sought to prevent vigorous anti-corruption investigations of his closest allies and supporters. Following recent political fallout from U.S.-backed corruption investigations in Afghanistan, some observers have questioned whether the benefits of strengthening Afghan anti-corruption institutions are worth the cost of aggravating the U.S. government's relationship with Karzai.[25]

High Office of Oversight

In August 2008 Karzai, with reported Bush Administration prodding, set up the "High Office of Oversight for the Implementation of Anti-Corruption Strategy" that is commonly referred to as the High Office of Oversight (HOO). This entity has the power to identify and refer corruption cases to state prosecutors, and to catalogue the overseas assets of Afghan officials. In his November 19, 2009, inaugural address, Karzai announced the upgrading of the HOO by increasing its scope of authority and resources. On March 18, 2010, Karzai, as promised during the January 28, 2010, international meeting on Afghanistan in London, issued a decree giving the High Office of Oversight direct power to investigate corruption cases rather than just refer them to other offices. The U.S. government gave the HOO about $1 million in assistance during FY2009, and its performance was audited by SIGAR in December 2009. The audit found deficiencies in the capacity and independence of the HOO but noted that it was still relatively new and emerging as an institution.[26]

---

[25] Mark Mazzetti, "As Time Passes, the Goals Shrink," *New York Times*, September 12, 2010; Greg Miller, "U.S. Anti-Graft Effort," *Washington Post*, September 10, 2010.

[26] Office of the Special Inspector General for Afghanistan Reconstruction (SIGAR), "Afghanistan's High Office of Oversight Needs Significantly Strengthened Authority, Independence, and Donor Support to Become an Effective Anti-Corruption Institution, Report No. 10-2, December 16, 2009.

Counter Narcotics Tribunal

This body was established by a July 2005 Karzai decree; it was proposed by then Supreme Court Chief Justice Fazl Ahmad Shinwari. The Tribunal remains under the Supreme Court's jurisdiction. The prosecutions of drug traffickers are tried at the Counter Narcotics Tribunal (CNT) following investigation by a Criminal Justice Task Force (CJTF). Together the two units have 65 Afghan prosecutors and investigators. [27]

Anti-Corruption Tribunal and Anti-Corruption Unit

These investigative and prosecutory bodies have been established by decree. Eleven judges have been appointed to the Anti-Corruption Tribunal (ACT), which operates under the jurisdiction of the Supreme Court. The Tribunal tries cases referred by an Anti-Corruption Unit (ACU) of the Afghan Attorney General's Office (AGO). According to testimony before the House Appropriations Committee (State and Foreign Operations Subcommittee) by Ambassador Richard Holbrooke on July 28, 2010, the ACT has received 79 cases from the ACU and is achieving a conviction rate of 90%. This Tribunal also is under the jurisdiction of the Supreme Court. Amid heightened tensions between the U.S. government and President Karzai in mid-2010 over corruption investigations, mentors from the Department of Justice (DOJ) were required to temporarily suspend their support to the ACU. [28]

Major Crimes Task Force and Sensitive Investigative Unit

Two key investigative bodies have been established since 2008. The most prominent is the Major Crimes Task Force (MCTF), tasked with investigating public corruption, organized crime, and kidnapping. A headquarters for the MCTF was inaugurated on February 25, 2010. According to the Federal Bureau of Investigation (FBI) press release that day, the MTCF is Afghan led but it is funded and mentored by the FBI, the U.S. Drug Enforcement Administration (DEA), the U.S. Marshals Service (USMS), Britain's Serious Organised Crime Agency, the Australian Federal Police, the European Union Police Mission in Afghanistan, and the U.S.-led training mission for Afghan forces. The MCTF currently has 169 investigators working on 36 cases, according to Amb. Holbrooke's July 28, 2010 testimony.

A related body is the Sensitive Investigative Unit (SIU), run by several dozen Afghan police officers, vetted and trained by the DEA. [29] It is this body that led the arrest in August 2010 of a Karzai National Security Council aide, Mohammad Zia Salehi on charges of soliciting a bribe from the large New Ansari money trading firm in exchange for ending a money-laundering investigation of the firm. The middle of the night arrest prompted Karzai, by his own acknowledgment on August 22, 2010, to obtain Salehi's release (although he still faces prosecution) and to establish a commission to place the MCTF and SIU under closer Afghan government control. Following U.S. criticism that Karzai is protecting his aides (Salehi reportedly has been involved in bringing Taliban figures to Afghanistan for conflict settlement

---

[27] U.S. Department of State, International Narcotics Control Strategy Report, 2009.

[28] Matthew Rosenberg and Maria Abi-Habib, "Afghan Prosecutors' Mentors Face New Curbs," *Wall Street Journal*, September 13, 2010.

[29] Ron Nordland and Mark Mazzetti, "Graft Dispute in Afghanistan is Test for U.S.," *New York Times*, August 24, 2010.

talks), Karzai pledged to visiting Senate Foreign Relations Committee Chairman John Kerry on August 20, 2010, that the MCTF and SIU would be allowed to perform their work without political interference.[30]

Traditional Justice Mechanisms

Afghans turn often to local, informal mechanisms such as local *shuras* or *jirgas* run by *mullahs, mawlawis* (highly qualified Islamic scholars), or other local elders or individuals with religious standing. The traditional justice sector often is used to adjudicate disputes involving local property, familial or local disputes, or personal status issues. Some estimates say that the majority of cases are decided in the informal justice system (see **Figure 3**). Recent surveys also show that the proportion of respondents who take cases to traditional mechanisms has increased while the proportion of those taking cases to state courts has fallen.[31] This is widely attributed not only to lack of trust of the formal justice system but also to the logistical difficulty and security concerns inherent in traveling to major population centers where the formal system's infrastructure (courts) is located. The non-governmental dispute resolution bodies also are widely considered more responsive and timelier in resolving cases,[32] particularly those types of cases that are usually brought to these local decision bodies.

Figure 3. Population Survey Results on the Informal Justice Sector

Responses to the Question "Have You Turned to Other Non-State Justice Providers to Resolve [a] Problem; If Yes, Who Were They?"

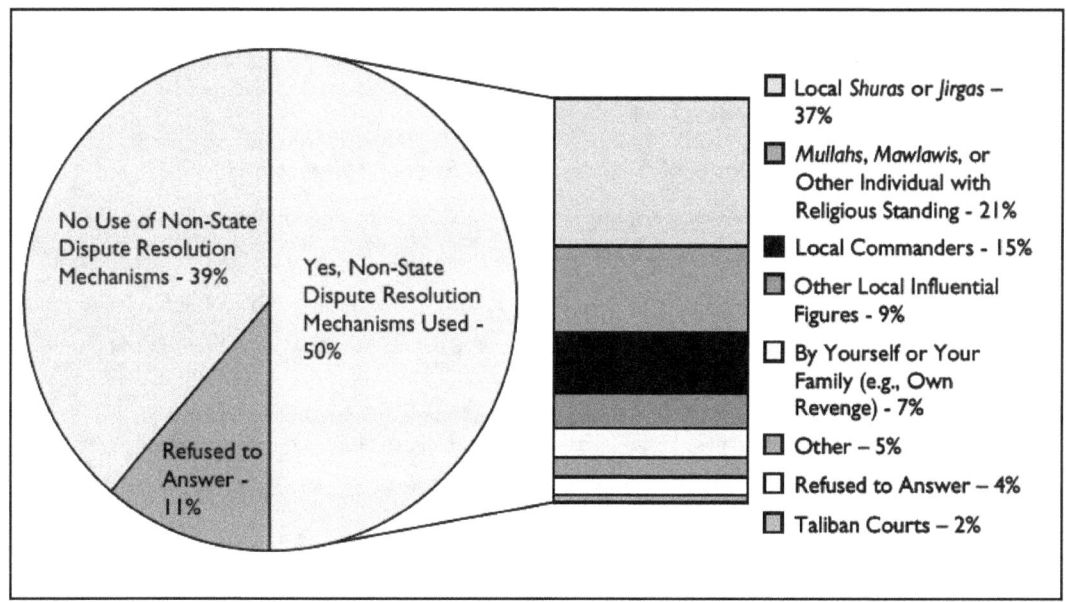

Source: CRS graphic of data from Integrity Watch Afghanistan, "Afghan Perceptions and Experiences of Corruption: A National Survey 2010," 2010, pp. 76-77.

---

[30] Ibid.

[31] The Asia Foundation, "Afghanistan in 2009: A Survey of the Afghan People," 2009, pp. 11, 93.

[32] Ibid, p. 89.

In the informal sector, Afghans can usually expect traditional practices of dispute resolution to prevail, including those practiced by Pashtuns. Some of these customs include traditional forms of apology ("*nanawati*" and "*shamana*") and compensation for wrongs done. These and other justice and dispute resolution mechanisms are discussed at http://www.khyber.org/articles/2004/JirgaRestorativeJustice.shtml.

Among the main criticisms is that the informal justice system is dominated almost exclusively by males. Some informal justice *shuras* take place in Taliban controlled territory, and some Afghans may prefer Taliban-run *shuras* when doing so means they will be judged by members of their own tribe or tribal confederation.

Genesis of ROL Strategies in Afghanistan: A Brief History

Afghan and international efforts to strengthen ROL and the justice sector in Afghanistan are held together by a series of overlapping and evolving strategic frameworks.[33] Justice sector strategy guidance is outlined in several Afghan strategic documents, including the 2008 *Afghanistan National Development Strategy* (ANDS), the *National Justice Sector Strategy*, *National Justice Program*, and most recently the 2010 *ANDS Prioritization and Implementation Plan*. Collectively, these documents lay out the key ROL objectives of the Afghan government, steps for implementation, and a framework for international donors to support Afghanistan's ROL sector. Separately, the U.S. government maintains a corresponding set of overlapping and evolving strategic frameworks for its civilian and military support to Afghanistan, which include ROL elements.

Chronology of Afghan Justice Sector Milestones

December 2001	Bonn Agreement signed; establishment of the Interim Administration
May 2002	Judicial Commission established with 16 Afghan legal scholars or practitioners
June 2002	Emergency Loya Jirga results in the establishment of a Transitional Administration
September 2002	Group of Eight Donor Conference held in Rome on judicial reform and transitional justice
November 2002	New 12-member Judicial Commission is mandated by decree; the Judicial Commission completes a detailed national plan for the justice sector
December 2002	Donor Conference held in Rome on Justice sector results in a total of $30 million pledged
Mid-2003	Authority over prisons transferred from the Afghan Ministry of Interior to the Ministry of Justice
January 2004	Constitutional Loya Jirga results in approval of a new Afghan Constitution
August 2005	Kabul Conference held at which the multilateral Consultative Group on Justice unveils a justice-sector plan called Justice For All
December 2005	The Bonn Agreement officially ends; the bicameral National Assembly opens

---

[33] The U.S. government strategies will be discussed subsequently in the section entitled U.S. Framework for Justice Sector Reform in Afghanistan.

February 2006	Afghanistan Compact and an interim Afghanistan National Development Strategy agreed to at the London Conference
May 2006	Afghan Supreme Court reports that one-third of the 1,415 official judges in Afghanistan have higher education qualifications
October 2006	International donor nations establish the International Coordination Group on Justice Reform, co-chaired by the United Nations Assistance Mission in Afghanistan and Italy, the original "lead nation" under the Bonn Agreement for justice sector reform
December 2006	Donor meeting held in Dubai on Afghanistan ROL coordination; United Nations Security Council describes the establishment of ROL and good governance in Afghanistan as "a matter of highest priority"
July 2007	Ministerial-Level International Conference on the ROL in Afghanistan in Rome results in donor pledges of $360 million over five years
June 2008	The Afghan National Development Strategy (ANDS) launched at the Paris Donor Conference; subsumed under the ANDS is the Afghan National Justice Sector Strategy and the Afghan National Justice Program
July 2010	In a follow-on to the January 2010 London Conference in Kabul, the Afghan government outlined its security and development goals for the next several years, including those related to governance and ROL

Transitional Justice Under the Bonn Agreement

Strategic efforts to strengthen ROL in Afghanistan began in 2001 following the United Nations-facilitated Bonn Conference, which culminated in an agreement that established an Afghan Interim Authority, as well as an interim legal framework and judicial system, which outlined steps to re-establish a permanent governance structure in Afghanistan.[34] Under the Bonn Agreement, a Judicial Reform Commission was assigned the responsibility to rebuild the Afghan justice sector and strengthen ROL.[35] To support the Judicial Reform Commission's efforts, Italy was assigned the lead donor nation role for judicial administration and the detention and corrections system.[36]

In the initial years following the 2001 Bonn Agreement, progress in the strengthening of the justice sector under the Judicial Reform Commission, as well as in the implementation of ROL assistance projects under the lead donor nation framework, was widely viewed as halting and under-resourced. In 2002 and 2003, the United Nations reported problems in the functioning of the Commission and in its inability to work collaboratively with other aspects of the justice sector, including the Ministry of Justice and the Supreme Court.[37] Due to reported "competing

---

[34] In accordance with the Bonn Agreement, multilateral security and development support to Afghanistan was provided through the establishment of the U.N. Security Council-mandated International Security Assistance Force (ISAF) in 2001 and U.N. Assistance Mission in Afghanistan (UNAMA) in 2002.

[35] United Nations Security Council and General Assembly, Report of the Secretary-General, "The Situation in Afghanistan and Its Implications for International Peace and Security," A/57/762-S/2003/333, March 18, 2003, p. 10.

[36] Police and counternarcotics assistance efforts, which have been viewed as separate but related components of the justice sector, were assigned to Germany and the United Kingdom respectively. While the lead nation concept was eventually discarded in favor of a more multi-sectoral, multinational approach to Afghan reconstruction, police training and counternarcotics support programs reportedly continue to be conducted and evaluated largely independently from other justice sector and ROL efforts. See U.S. Department of State and the Broadcasting Board of Governors, OIG, "Department of State-Department of Defense, Interagency Assessment of Afghanistan Police Training and Readiness," Report No. ISP-IQO-07-07, November 2006; U.S. Department of State and the Broadcasting Board of Governors, OIG, "Interagency Assessment of Counternarcotics Program in Afghanistan," Report No. ISP-I-07-34, July 2007.

[37] Related to the reported problems of the Judicial Reform Commission, the membership of the Commission was (continued...)

---

fiscal priorities" and low levels of donor support in the justice sector generally, but particularly pronounced in the corrections sector, minimal progress reportedly took place in the initial years.[38] Further, disconnects in donor coordination and commitments across sectors contributed to views that progress in the justice sector was lagging behind other sectors.

The Afghan Constitution and Formal Justice Sector Challenges

Between 2004 and 2006, a series of governance milestones took place, which, while not necessarily resulting in sustained progress in the justice sector, nevertheless established a baseline for the eventual future direction of Afghan justice sector support. First, the Constitutional Loya Jirga concluded in January 2004 with the signing of the new Afghan Constitution. With the establishment of a formal Afghan government following approval of the Constitution, donor nations could begin to support the development of a formal Afghan government justice sector. At the end of 2004, national elections were held and in December 2004 President Karzai was inaugurated. December 2005 marked the end of the Bonn Agreement and the opening of an elected, bicameral National Assembly. In February 2006, the London Conference on Afghanistan culminated with the Afghanistan Compact and the *interim Afghanistan National Development Strategy* (iANDS), which, combined, set out strategic priorities and plans for Afghan development. One of the three principal pillars of the Compact and Strategy was "governance, ROL, and human rights." The concept of lead donor nations was also dropped at the 2006 London Conference.[39] During this timeframe, the U.S. government became the largest contributor to programs in support of ROL and justice sector capacity building.

By the end of 2006, it had become increasingly clear to many in the donor community that serious gaps remained in the Afghan justice sector. The United Nations described the Afghan justice system in 2006 as suffering from a lack of sufficiently qualified judges, prosecutors, and lawyers, as well as limited by the absence of necessary physical infrastructure to administer justice fairly and effectively.[40] Earlier that year, the Afghan Supreme Court issued a report on judicial education that highlighted the system-wide absence of fundamental judicial capabilities: only about one-third of the 1,415 sitting judges in Afghanistan were found to possess higher education qualifications.[41] Judicial officials had become targets for assassination, compounding problems of recruitment and retention. Prison riots and attacks as well as incidents of escaped prisoners underlined the security vulnerabilities of the corrections system. According to observers, well-connected prisoners were often released when relatives complained about their incarceration, leading to a perception that justice in Afghanistan was selectively applied. Other observers described low levels of public confidence in the justice sector, with due process

---

(...continued)

reviewed during the 2002-2003 timeframe and, by Presidential decree, was reduced from a 16-member body to a 12-member body. United Nations Security Council, Report of the Secretary-General, "The Situation in Afghanistan and Its Implications for International Peace and Security," S/2003/1212, December 30, 2003, p. 6.

[38] United Nations Security Council and General Assembly, Report of the Secretary-General, "The Situation in Afghanistan and Its Implications for International Peace and Security," A/58/868-S/2004/634, August 12, 2004, p. 11; U.S. Department of State and Broadcasting Board of Governors, OIG, Report No. ISP-I-08-09, January 2008, p. 4.

[39] U.S. Department of State and Broadcasting Board of Governors, OIG, Report No. ISP-I-08-09, January 2008, p. 4.

[40] United Nations, General Assembly and Security Council, Report of the Secretary-General, "The Situation in Afghanistan and its Implications for International Peace and Security: Emergency International Assistance for Peace, Normalcy, and Reconstruction of War-Stricken Afghanistan," A/60.712 – S/2006/145, March 7, 2006, p. 6.

[41] Ibid, p. 11.

---

systematically undermined by lengthy pretrial detentions, and the absence of legal defense representation.

By December 2006, a United Nations Security Council mission to Afghanistan sought to emphasize the perceived importance of prioritizing justice sector support, stating:

> As a matter of highest priority, the mission urges the Government of Afghanistan with the support of its international partners to establish rule of law and good governance throughout the country. To this end, the mission encourages the Government to take immediate steps to strengthen justice sector institutions and provincial government, including the replacement of corrupt officials and local power brokers. In these efforts, the Government must enjoy the united support of the international community and adequate resources. More effective mechanisms for strategic planning, funding and coordination of rule of law programmes among international donors and agencies at the national and provincial levels are required. There is also the need to address the problem of endemic corruption within the judiciary and for a comprehensive review of judicial service. The mission calls upon donors to increase the coherence and scale of assistance in the development of Afghanistan's human capital, with special priority to be given to the reform of the country's civil service.[42]

The Afghanistan National Development Strategy and Justice Sector Donor Support

Although donor contributions for justice sector assistance remained limited, compared to other sectors, 2007 was marked by previously unprecedented pledges. At the 2007 Ministerial-Level International Conference on ROL in Afghanistan, hosted in Rome, Italy, donors pledged to contribute $360 million over five years to justice sector reform.

In 2008, the Afghan government released its final *Afghanistan National Development Strategy* (ANDS), as well as supplemental details for justice sector development in the *National Justice Sector Strategy* (NJSS) and *National Justice Program* (NJP). The ANDS sets out several ROL objectives to be met by the end of 2010. Objectives included

- completing the basic legal framework, including civil, criminal, and commercial law;

- rehabilitating the physical justice sector infrastructure;

- establishing active and operational formal justice sector institutions in all 34 Afghan provinces;

- reviewing and reforming oversight procedures related to corruption, lack of due process, and other miscarriages of the law; and

- implementing reforms to strengthen the professionalism, credibility, and integrity of justice sector institutions.[43]

---

[42] United Nations Security Council, Report of the Security Council Mission to Afghanistan, 11 to 16 November 2006, S/2006/935, December 4, 2006, p. 11.

[43] DOD, Report on Progress Toward Security, January 2009, p. 54.

The *National Justice Sector Strategy* (NJSS) is an element of the ANDS and sets out additional justice sector development goals to be met by 2013. The *National Justice Program* (NJP) set forth steps to implement the goals of the ANDS and the NJSS, using a combination of Afghan and bilateral and multilateral donor funds to develop and reform the justice system.

Following the 2010 London Conference on Afghanistan in January, the international community relationship with the Afghan government has shifted into a new "transition" phase. In this new phase, international actors will continue to play a supporting role, but responsibility for Afghan security and development will rest with the Afghan government. In July 2010, a follow-on to the London Conference took place in Kabul, during which the Afghan government outlined its security and development goals for the next several years. Included among such goals were several related to governance and ROL. These goals were set forth in an updated supplement to the 2008 ANDS, called the *ANDS Prioritization and Implementation Plan*.[44] This emerging phase is marked by two key trends in justice sector support efforts: (1) an increased concern about the extent of corruption within the Afghan government and (2) an increased interest about how to address the informal justice sector.[45]

The U.S. Response

Promoting ROL and justice sector development is part of the broader effort to increase the legitimacy of Afghan governance and institutions. Emphasis on this aspect of the overall U.S. strategy for stabilizing Afghanistan appears to be increasing under the Obama Administration, particularly as the Karzai government continues to be challenged by widespread perceptions of corruption. Specifics regarding the implementation of such broad ROL goals, however, continue to evolve.

Justice sector assistance programs in Afghanistan have historically centered on efforts to build the capacity of the courts and justice agencies (e.g., Supreme Court, Ministry of Justice, and Attorney General's Office). These efforts include support to develop the physical infrastructure of the justice system, as well as training, mentoring, and other forms of capacity building. While the police are considered a component of the justice sector, assistance to the law enforcement sector in Afghanistan has historically been implemented and evaluated separately from other ROL programs. A similar explanation applies to counternarcotics efforts in Afghanistan, which also have ROL dimensions.

More recent efforts have sought to expand upon existing programs to increase Afghan access to justice at the provincial and district level as well as to develop linkages between the formal and informal justice sector. Since approximately 2004, when the first formal U.S. government ROL programs were first implemented, ROL programs have evolved to include greater emphasis on the informal justice sector. This is a development that is both considered central to the counterinsurgency (COIN) strategy in Afghanistan and controversial among some for its lack of

---

[44] Under the proposed National Program for Justice For All, two key goals include improving delivery of justice sector services and expanding access to justice. See also the Kabul International Conference on Afghanistan, Afghanistan National Development Strategy, *Prioritization and Implementation Plan: Mid 2010 – Mid 2013*, for consideration at the 14th Meeting of the Joint Coordination and Monitoring Board, p. 16.

[45] See for example White House, Office of the Press Secretary, President Barack Obama, "Remarks by the President on a New Strategy for Afghanistan and Pakistan," March 27, 2009; and U.S. Department of State and Broadcasting Board of Governors, OIG, "Embassy Kabul, Afghanistan," Report No. ISP-I-06-13A, February 2010.

uniform adherence to international human rights standards and for other reasons. However, the traditional justice system is difficult for international donors to influence because it is practiced in areas that are not under government control or that are difficult to access.

Strategic Guidance

In February 2010, the State Department issued the *Afghanistan and Pakistan Regional Stabilization Strategy*, which includes "enhancing Afghan rule of law" as one of its nine "key initiatives" for Afghanistan.[46] The 2010 *Stabilization Strategy* identifies five major ROL program objectives including strengthening traditional justice; capacity building for the formal justice sector;[47] corrections sector support; enhanced access to formal justice; and enhanced and focused outreach. Justice sector reform is also featured as a policy priority in the *U.S. Counternarcotics Strategy for Afghanistan*, last updated in March 2010.[48]

Although not available publicly, the Administration also maintains other strategies and guidance related to ROL and the justice sector, including, but not limited to a *U.S. Strategy for Rule of Law in Afghanistan* and a *U.S. Strategy for Anti-Corruption in Afghanistan*. According to the State Department, the *Rule of Law Strategy* is composed of four pillars, or goals:[49]

- **Pillar 1:** Tackle the pervasive culture of impunity and improve and expand access to the state justice sector, by increasing capacity and reducing corruption in the justice sector's institutions;

- **Pillar 2:** Support corrections reform;

- **Pillar 3:** Provide security and space for traditional justice systems to re-emerge organically in areas cleared of the Taliban and engage closely at the grassroots level to ensure dispute resolution needs in the local communities are being met; and

- **Pillar 4:** Build the leadership capacity of the Afghan government's justice sector, and civil society generally.

The 2010 *Afghanistan and Pakistan Regional Stabilization Strategy* followed on several prior strategic plans under the Obama Administration, which also emphasized ROL and related justice sector support programs. These included the 2009 *Integrated Civilian-Military Campaign Plan* and several earlier speeches by President Obama on the future direction of U.S. efforts in Afghanistan.

The August 2009 *Integrated Civilian-Military Campaign Plan*, jointly released by the Departments of State and Defense, established a framework for the coordination of both civilian and military activities in Afghanistan.[50] This *Campaign Plan* provided guidance on how to

---

[46] U.S. Department of State, Office of the Special Representative for Afghanistan and Pakistan (S/RAP), Afghanistan and Pakistan Regional Stabilization Strategy, updated February 24, 2010.

[47] Specifically, the courts, Attorney General's Office, Anti-Corruption Unit, Major Crimes Task Force, Ministry of Justice, and the national case management system.

[48] U.S. Department of State, Bureau of South and Central Asian Affairs (SCA), *U.S. Counternarcotics Strategy for Afghanistan*, March 24, 2010.

[49] U.S. Department of State response to CRS, June 2010.

[50] U.S. Departments of State and Defense, *U.S. Government Integrated Civilian-Military Campaign Plan for Support to* (continued...)

execute the U.S. mission in Afghanistan over the next three years, with particular emphasis on the immediate 12 to 18 month time frame. Among its goals, the *Campaign Plan* outlined 11 "transformative effects" or thematic missions to achieve, including improving access to justice; expansion of accountable and transparent governance; and countering the nexus of insurgency, narcotics, corruption, and criminality.

On March 27, 2009, President Obama announced the key findings of a 60-day high-level review of U.S. efforts in Afghanistan. Cornerstone elements of the strategic review included an increased emphasis on counterinsurgency (COIN) and on strengthening the legitimacy of the Afghan government through increased civilian assistance. Support would occur not only at the national level, but also at the provincial and local government level.[51] This announcement followed President Obama's speech at West Point on December 1, 2009, which reinforced the goal of strengthening the justice sector and ROL in Afghanistan and highlighted the importance of combating corruption and delivery of services through an increasingly resourced and combined military and civilian effort. [52]

U.S. Policy Coordination

U.S. government agencies that are involved in ROL-related programming and policymaking in Afghanistan include the following:

- **State Department:** particularly the Office of the Special Representative for Afghanistan and Pakistan (S/RAP), and the Bureaus of International Narcotics and Law Enforcement Affairs (INL) and South and Central Asian Affairs (SCA).

- **Department of Justice (DOJ):** particularly Justice Department attorneys, the Federal Bureau of Investigation (FBI), the Marshals Service (USMS), the Drug Enforcement Administration (DEA), and the Criminal Division's International Criminal Investigative Training Assistance Program (ICITAP).

- **U.S. Agency for International Development (USAID):** particularly the Bureau for Democracy, Conflict, and Humanitarian Assistance (DCHA) and the Asia Bureau.

- **Department of Defense (DOD):** particularly through the U.S. Forces-Afghanistan/International Security Assistance Force (USF-A/ISAF), North Atlantic Treaty Organization (NATO)-ISAF Training Mission-Afghanistan (NTM-A), U.S. Central Command (CENTCOM), Judge Advocate General's Corps (JAG), Combined Joint Task Force 101 (CJTF-101), and Combined Joint Interagency Task Force 435 (CJIATF-435).

- **Department of the Treasury:** particularly the Office of Technical Assistance (OTA).

(...continued)

Afghanistan, August 10, 2009.

[51] White House, White Paper of the Interagency Policy Group's Report on U.S. Policy Toward Afghanistan and Pakistan, March 27, 2009. See in particular pp. 3-4.

[52] White House, "Remarks by the President in Address to the Nation on the Way Forward in Afghanistan and Pakistan," Eisenhower Hall Theatre, United States Military Academy at West Point, West Point, New York, December 1, 2009.

- **Department of Homeland Security (DHS):** particularly Immigration and Customs Enforcement (ICE).

Given the multiplicity of U.S. entities involved, program and policy coordination has been an important aspect of ROL activities in Afghanistan. However, the history of ROL coordination in Afghanistan highlights the difficulties that policymakers encountered. In many ways, ROL policy coordination continues to be a work in progress.

Coordination Under the Bush Administration

Following the establishment of the Afghan Constitution in 2004, formal U.S. assistance projects in the justice sector expanded significantly and soon were so numerous and lacking in coordination that they risked "wasteful duplication and contradictory legal reform efforts."[53] According to a June 2008 report by the State Department's Office of the Inspector General (OIG), "So many different international partners and U.S. government agencies were working with so many different grantees and contractors that by 2004 serious questions were raised regarding how well the U.S. government and its allies were communicating with one another, coordinating their efforts, and monitoring their expenditures."[54]

Steps to address ROL coordination began roughly in 2005 with the establishment of a ROL coordinator position in Kabul. In November 2005, the U.S. Ambassador to Afghanistan requested a special ROL coordination office to be located within Embassy Kabul. In early 2006, a Special ROL Counselor, with the rank of Ambassador, was appointed, but held the position temporarily for approximately three months. In October 2006, the U.S. ROL coordinator position was filled on a permanent basis, with a deputy coordinator position filled in 2007.

The ROL coordinator became the lead voice and source of ROL information, communication, and guidance of the U.S. government in Afghanistan—both in international donor meetings dealing with ROL matters and with Afghan government officials on matters with judicial sector implications. The ROL coordinator also chaired a weekly meeting at the U.S. Embassy in Kabul, initially called the Special Committee for ROL and later, under the Obama Administration, renamed the ROL Working Group, to plan and coordinate U.S. government ROL activities.[55] The primary purpose of the ROL Working Group was to share information and update U.S. government agency representatives on their ROL activities and programming.

Coordination Under the Obama Administration

Several changes to ROL coordination have taken place since the beginning of the Obama Administration. In June 2009, a new Ambassador-rank position was created at the U.S. Embassy in Kabul, the Coordinating Director for Development and Economic Affairs (CDDEA). This position was intended to oversee all U.S. government non-military assistance to Afghanistan. The ROL coordinator thus became subsumed under the CDDEA. In July 2010, the CDDEA's portfolio was split to establish a separate Ambassador-rank position specifically for justice sector issues entitled the Coordinating Director of ROL and Law Enforcement (CDROLLE).

---

[53] DOD, *Rule of Law Handbook*, 2008, 2nd ed., p. 219.

[54] U.S. Department of State and Broadcasting Board of Governors, OIG, Report No. ISP-I-08-09, January 2008, p. 8.

[55] U.S. Department of State response to CRS request, June 17, 2010.

Coordinating Director of ROL and Law Enforcement

The CDROLLE position is currently held by Ambassador Hans Klemm, the former U.S. Ambassador to East Timor. Ambassador Klemm is the lead U.S. government representative for ROL policy in Afghanistan. The creation of the CDROLLE position represents the first time in which ROL issues are the core element of a portfolio handled by a permanent, Ambassador-rank official at the U.S. Embassy in Kabul. Under the CDROLLE directorate are representatives from the State Department's International Narcotics and Law Enforcement Affairs Bureau (INL), DOD, DOJ, FBI, DEA, Department of Homeland Security's Immigration and Customs Enforcement, and the U.S. Marshals Service.

Combined Joint Interagency Task Force 435 and the ROL Field Force

In parallel to the establishment of the CDROLLE position in July, the military established the Combined Joint Interagency Task Force 435 (CJIATF-435) at Camp Phoenix. CJIATF-435 is a follow-on to the Joint Task Force 435 (JTF-435), which began operations in January 2010 and was mainly focused on transitioning control of U.S. military detention operations in Afghanistan to the government of Afghanistan. CJIATF-435 expands upon existing detention and corrections-related activities, to focus also on the development of Afghan investigative, prosecutorial, and judicial capabilities. Subsumed under CJATIF-435 is a new entity called the ROL Field Force (ROLFF), commanded by Gen. Mark Martins. According to a press release, ROLFF's mission is "to provide essential field capabilities and security to Afghan, coalition, and civil-military ROL project teams in non-permissive areas of Afghanistan, in order to build Afghan criminal justice capacity and promote the legitimacy of the Afghan government."[56]

Interagency Planning and Implementation Team

Also newly established is the ROL Interagency Planning and Implementation Team (IPIT). This coordinating entity, co-located with CJIATF-435, is intended to facilitate the implementation of jointly-run civilian and military ROL programs.[57]

Coordination Outlook

While bureaucratic coordination on ROL issues has reportedly greatly improved, observers indicate that coordination across a sector as broad and multi-faceted as ROL will require ongoing upkeep and face ongoing challenges, according to some observers. Factors impeding ROL coordination include the continuous turnover of staff stationed in Afghanistan, as well as conflicting priorities, and differing operating time horizons and capabilities among the various entities involved in ROL efforts.[58] These factors are a challenge not only among and between U.S. government entities, but also among the other international donors involved in ROL assistance in Afghanistan. Changes to the current coordination mechanisms in place or the

---

[56] U.S. Department of Defense, Central Command, "Rule of Law Conference Brings Together Afghan, International Partners," September 29, 2010.

[57] U.S. Department of Defense, Central Command, "Rule of Law Conference Brings Together Afghan, International Partners," September 29, 2010.

[58] U.S. Department of State and Broadcasting Board of Governors, OIG, Report No. ISP-I-08-09, January 2008.

relative participation of various U.S. agencies involved in ROL efforts may occur under the new CDROLLE and CJIATF-435, as both entities evolve.

Civilian Outreach at the Provincial and District Levels

ROL programs have been mainly implemented at the national level in Kabul. More recently, U.S. efforts have focused on extending the reach of the U.S. civilian justice sector support efforts at the provincial and district levels.[59] The recent increased emphasis on expanding ROL at the provincial and district levels is in part a response to a perceived oversaturation of ROL advisors in Kabul and an absence of civilian ROL advisors elsewhere in Afghanistan, where approximately 90% of the populace resides.[60] In 2008, for example, U.S. government officials characterized the number of justice advisors in Kabul as having reached a "point of saturation" and that the baseline knowledge of the Afghan justice sector outside Kabul remained "fairly rudimentary."[61] Additionally, due largely to the security situation and lack of comparable civilian presence at the provincial and district levels of Afghanistan, the U.S. military was often the primary interface with Afghan officials on ROL issues outside Kabul.

To address such concerns, there has been a gradual expansion in the amount of ROL resources and, particularly since the 2009 announcement of a "civilian uplift," in the number of civilian ROL advisors in Afghanistan. Civilian funding for ROL efforts in Afghanistan has also increased in recent years. As part of the 2008 proposal for a "civilian uplift" to support provincial- and local-level capacity-building in Afghanistan, the number of U.S. government ROL advisors at U.S.-led provincial reconstruction teams (PRTs) and military task forces has increased to more than a dozen in 2010.[62] Additionally, State Department advisors from the INL Bureau are located at seven Regional Training Centers (RTCs) in Bamyan, Gardez, Herat, Jalalabad, Kandahar, Konduz, and Mazar-e-Sharif. Most recently, the U.S. military has established a ROL field force (ROLFF), whose mission is to support jointly implemented civilian and military ROL projects in the field, including in otherwise non-permissive areas of Afghanistan.[63]

Although the U.S. government does not have a permanent presence throughout all 34 Afghan provinces and 364 Afghan districts, there are several mechanisms in place to spread and expand

---

[59] White House, Office of the Press Secretary, President Barack Obama, "Remarks by the President on a New Strategy for Afghanistan and Pakistan," March 27, 2009; Karen De Young, "Civilians to Join Afghan Buildup," *The Washington Post*, March 19, 2009.

[60] See for example the proposal at the 2007 Rome Conference to establish a Provincial Justice Coordination Mechanism (PJCM). The proposal states that "while the international community is effectively expanding and coordinating justice sector assistance at the national level in Kabul, it has been largely ineffective at helping the Afghan Government project justice into the provinces."

[61] U.S. Department of State, INL Bureau, Assistant Secretary of State David Johnson Testimony, statement for the record for a hearing on "Oversight of U.S. Efforts to Train and Equip Police and Enhance the Justice Sector in Afghanistan," before the U.S. House of Representatives, Committee on Oversight and Government Reform, Subcommittee on National Security and Foreign Affairs June 18, 2008; U.S. Department of State and Broadcasting Board of Governors, OIG, Deputy Assistant Inspector General for Inspections, Francis Ward, statement for the record for the same hearing. Ward continued: "There are questions about the actual number and qualifications of prosecutors and corrections officials, the number of cases that are going through the courts and the true conditions of the facilities of the justice sector."

[62] U.S. Department of State and Broadcasting Board of Governors, OIG, Report No. ISP-I-06-13A, February 2010.

[63] U.S. Department of Defense, Central Command, "Rule of Law Conference Brings Together Afghan, International Partners," September 29, 2010.

ROL programming beyond Kabul and into the provinces and districts. They are variously led or funded by the U.S. government, the Afghan government, or the United Nations.

Selected Outreach Mechanisms

Provincial Reconstruction Teams (PRTs)

PRTs, introduced in Afghanistan in 2002, are enclaves of U.S. or partner military forces and civilian officials that support reconstruction and assisting stabilization efforts. They perform activities ranging from resolving local disputes to coordinating local reconstruction projects, although most PRTs in combat-heavy areas focus mostly on counterinsurgency (COIN) and have historically played a limited role in ROL. PRTs have reportedly increased their participation in ROL programming, particularly among those under U.S. command since 2007; since the beginning of the Obama Administration's civilian surge, more than a dozen ROL coordinator positions have been established at PRTs.

Regional Training Centers (RTCs)

Although traditionally focused on police training activities, ROL programs under the State Department and USAID also conduct justice sector and corrections-related training through the seven RTCs located across Afghanistan, including in Kandahar, Kunduz, Herat, Jalalabad, Gardez, Mazar-e Sharif, and Bamyan. Justice sector staff from the INL Bureau is permanently located at these RTCs.

ROL Field Force (ROLFF)

The ROLFF is a new entity under CJIATF-435 established in mid-2010. Led by Gen. Mark Martins, its mission is to support Afghan, coalition, and civil-military ROL project teams in non-permissive areas of Afghanistan.

Provincial Justice Coordination Mechanism (PJCM)

First proposed at the 2007 Rome Conference on Justice and ROL in Afghanistan, and later launched in 2008, the provincial justice coordination mechanism is a joint United Nations Development Program (UNDP) and United Nations Assistance Mission to Afghanistan (UNAMA) project that is funded by the United States, Canada, Italy, and Germany, and designed to assist the Afghan government in expanding ROL beyond Kabul and improve the delivery of justice assistance in the provinces. Through the PJCM, permanent field units are located in seven in major population centers outside Kabul, including Kandahar, Kunduz, Herat, Jalalabad, Gardez, Mazar-e Sharif, and Bamyan.

Provincial Justice Conferences (PJCs)

The State Department organizes periodic multi-day conferences in various Afghan provinces that bring prosecutors, judges, police, corrections officers, and defense attorneys together for training and interaction. Often, they are held on the premises of a provincial governor's compound. Since 2006, provincial justice conferences, with follow-up trainings, have been held in the following provinces: Bamyan, Kunduz, Ghazni, Logar, Panjshir, Kapisa, Paktia, Kunar, Badghis, Nangarhar, Laghman, Helmand, and Wardak.

Independent National Legal Training Centers (INLTCs)

The U.S. government has supported the creation and development of the INLTC, a law library currently operating in Kabul. With current USAID funding, the goal is to support the development of at least six additional law libraries in other parts of Afghanistan, particularly in the south and east, to promote better access to the law and support training for justice sector professionals on how to conduct legal research.

Source: Congressional Research Service.

Funding for U.S. ROL Programs in Afghanistan

U.S. assistance to Afghanistan's justice sector is provided in the form of justice sector training, mentoring, equipping, and infrastructure building. Justice sector assistance is funded through both civilian and military appropriations vehicles and implemented by a combination of U.S. government agencies, NGOs and private contractors. Civilian expenditures on ROL support in Afghanistan have increased from an estimated $7 million in FY2002 to an estimated $411 million in FY2010, totaling $904 million from FY2002 to FY2010. In 2008, the State Department stated in testimony to Congress that Afghanistan's justice sector would require more than $600 million worth of additional assistance over the next five years. Other U.S. government reports indicate that $600 million might underestimate the likely costs, given degradations in the Afghan security environment since the estimate was made.[64]

U.S. ROL funding for programs in Afghanistan, including both civilian and military components, is difficult to identify and quantify. As a 2008 inspection review of ROL programs in Afghanistan by the State Department's Office of the Inspector General (OIG) explains:

> Funding for the ROL program in Afghanistan is split among several U.S. government agencies. There is no one place where all funds spent specifically on ROL can be identified. ROL program funding is often multiyear and is combined with other programs such as police training and corrections facilities, which often make identification of specific costs difficult. ROL programs are also funded by the UN, other bilateral donors, and a variety of NGOs. The result is that there is currently no way to readily identify ROL funding and subsequently identify duplicate programs, overlapping programs, or programs conflicting with each other. Afghans, while seemingly eager to embrace ROL, are confused by the variety of programs implemented specifically by INL, USAID, and the U.S. military units in Afghanistan. Funding figures from one source may not match other Department or agency funding matrices identifying funds that are ROL specific.[65]

Most non-Defense Department foreign assistance for ROL activities in Afghanistan is funded by from two foreign aid accounts: Economic Support Fund (ESF) and International Narcotics Control and Law Enforcement (INCLE). DOD ROL efforts are funded through the Commander's Emergency Response Program (CERP) and the Afghanistan Security Forces Fund (ASFF), among other sources.

At least a few estimates for total U.S. government spending on ROL assistance are available. These estimates, however, suffer from several various limitations, which include

- differing or unclear criteria for what constitutes ROL programming, such as whether police, corrections, or justice-related counternarcotics assistance are included, and whether general governance capacity building assistance and support for human rights are included;[66]

---

[64] U.S. Department of State, INL Bureau, Assistant Secretary of State David Johnson Testimony, statement for the record for a hearing on "Oversight of U.S. Efforts to Train and Equip Police and Enhance the Justice Sector in Afghanistan," before the U.S. House of Representatives, Committee on Oversight and Government Reform, Subcommittee on National Security and Foreign Affairs June 18, 2008. For concern regarding the possible underestimation of the cost, see DOD, Report on Progress Toward Security and Stability in Afghanistan, January 2009. See also U.S. Government Accountability Office (GAO), "Afghanistan: Key Issues of Congressional Oversight," Report No. GAO-09-473SP, April 2009, p. 25. This GAO report shows the Afghan National Development Strategy's overall funding and expenditures between 2008 and 2013 and highlights the total shortfalls between government revenue and planned costs.

[65] U.S. Department of State and Broadcasting Board of Governors, OIG, Deputy Assistant Inspector General for Inspections, Francis Ward, statement for the record for a hearing on "Oversight of U.S. Efforts to Train and Equip Police and Enhance the Justice Sector in Afghanistan," before the U.S. House of Representatives, Committee on Oversight and Government Reform, Subcommittee on National Security and Foreign Affairs June 18, 2008.

[66] The 2008 OIG report, for example, states that "although large sums of money are being directed towards efforts in Afghanistan that contribute to creating a just and secure society, it is not always clear which of these funds can be described as purely 'rule of law.'" U.S. Department of State and Broadcasting Board of Governors, OIG, Report No. ISP-I-08-09, January 2008.

- incomplete or non-comparable estimates of ROL programming across agencies, due to the varying inclusion or omission of staffing and administrative program management costs, differing appropriations vehicles, as well as changes in foreign aid tracking methodologies since the beginning of ROL assistance in Afghanistan; and[67]

- the unclear inclusion or omission of potential sources of ROL assistance funding and ROL assistance-related costs, particularly for U.S. military and law enforcement funding sources.[68]

As the 2008 OIG report explains, "the U.S. government, through several agencies, is funding many programs related to ROL.... However, no one source seems to have a clear picture of the scope of U.S. expenditure in this field."[69]

Overall, these estimates indicate that U.S. assistance to the Afghan justice sector has grown gradually since FY2002, accelerating in recent years to become the largest foreign donor in this sector (see **Figure 4**). In FY2002, the U.S. Government Accountability Office (GAO) estimates that the U.S. government provided $7 million for ROL programming. From FY2002 through FY2007, U.S. assistance totaled a combined $160 million for ROL programming. In the next two fiscal years, U.S. assistance for ROL in Afghanistan more than doubled prior expenditures.

---

[67] The 2008 OIG report, for example, states that tracking justice sector funds and programs are challenged by the differing funding mechanisms used, such as multi-year and supplemental funds. The report also indicates that with respect to State Department foreign aid, justice sector programs prior to FY2006/7 may include redundant and overlapping totals, due to double-counted overhead and staffing costs. Also, in 2006, the State Department revised its foreign assistance planning and tracking system through the Office of the Director of Foreign Assistance, which revised definitions and program descriptions for aid accounts. As part of this, beginning in FY2007, the State Department revised the methodology by which ROL activities were identified, coordinated, and evaluated. Ibid, p. 1.

[68] The 2008 OIG report, for example, states that there is "no way to determine what the many different elements of DOD (some under direct DOD command, some under NATO), were spending specifically on ROL, but the current military leadership in Afghanistan briefed the team that implementing ROL programs was important to them." Ibid.

[69] Ibid, p. 2.

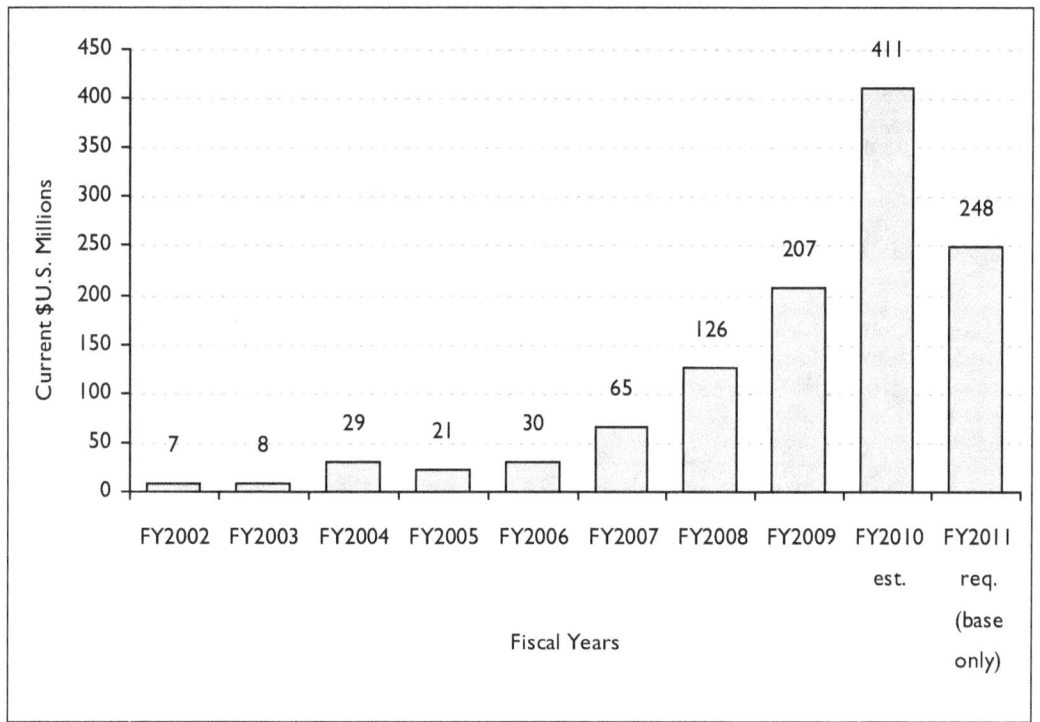

Figure 4. U.S. Civilian Funding for Afghan ROL Assistance, FY2002-FY2010 and FY2011 Request

Source: U.S. Government Accountability Office (GAO), "Afghanistan: Key Issues of Congressional Oversight," Report No. GAO-09-473SP, April 2009, p. 4, for FY2002-FY2005 and U.S. Department of State response to CRS request, August 12, 2010, for the other fiscal years.

Notes: Note that the State Department's methodology for calculating foreign assistance changed beginning in FY2006. It is unclear if earlier years include comparable data. This chart does not include funding or costs directly provided or incurred by the Defense Department or U.S. law enforcement agencies without State Department or USAID reimbursement. For FY2006 on, funding included is "program area 2.1: "ROL and Human Rights".

Table 1. Funding for ROL Assistance to Afghanistan provided the State Department's INL Bureau

in current $U.S. millions

	FY06	FY07	FY08	FY09	FY10	FY11
Justice System Development	8	47	59.6	67.4	145	98
Corrections System Development	18.5	8	31.9	96	150	80
Counternarcotics Justice and Anti-Corruption	0	0	3	4	33	12
Protect Women and Girls	0	0	0	14	0	0
INL Total for Administration of Justice Programs	**26.5**	**55**	**94.5**	**181.4**	**328**	**190**

Sources: U.S. Department of State, Bureau for International Narcotics and Law Enforcement Affairs (INL), Program and Budget Guide, FY2008; U.S. Department of State response to CRS request, August 12, 2010, for FY2008 to present.

Notes: FY2010 is base estimate and supplemental request; FY2011 is base request only. Other years include supplemental appropriations.

International donors also provided financial contributions to ROL efforts in Afghanistan. At the 2007 Rome Conference on ROL in Afghanistan, for example, international donors, other than the United States, pledged to contribute $83 million in new ROL assistance to be administered by the World Bank, which exceeded prior international commitments to contribute $82 million for ROL assistance in Afghanistan. The U.S. government pledged $15 million at the 2007 Rome Conference. It remains unclear, however, whether U.S. and other donor contributions will cover the estimated Afghan need for ROL assistance.

Scope of U.S. ROL Programs in Afghanistan

The scope of U.S. ROL programs in Afghanistan is broad and inherently multi-disciplinary. The following sections break down such programs into three categories: major justice sector programs, selected other justice sector programs, and cross cutting ROL programs. Major programs include the primary projects implemented by the Departments of State, Justice, and Defense, as well as USAID. The State Department, USAID, and DOD also fund several smaller projects to support Afghanistan's justice sector. These are described in the section on selected other justice sector projects. Additionally, multiple other U.S. efforts in Afghanistan have implications for the ROL. While these projects tend not to be described or defined as ROL programs, many observers would agree that the success of these projects is likely to impact the success of the major U.S.-funded justice sector programs.

Major Justice Sector Programs

The four major U.S. funded programs are the Judicial Sector Support Program (JSSP), the Corrections System Support Program (CSSP), the ROL Stabilization (RLS) Program, and the Senior Federal Prosecutors Program. JSSP, CSSP, and the Senior Federal Prosecutors Program are all managed and funded through the State Department's INL Bureau. The RLS program is a USAID-funded program that began in mid-2010 as a follow-on to USAID original ROL program, called the Afghanistan ROL Project (ARoLP). ARoLP ran from approximately October 2004 to June 2009. After roughly a year's hiatus, the expanded RLS program began. Unlike its predecessor, the RLS program has two sub-program elements, including one focused on the formal justice sector (mainly the Supreme Court) and a new, second component focused on the informal justice sector. DOD also funds multiple ROL projects. However, such efforts are not necessarily organized under a central program or project name.

Judicial Sector Support Program (JSSP)

The State Department's INL Bureau funds the majority of U.S. government justice sector support to Afghanistan through several programs.[70] INL's primary assistance program for such support is the Justice Sector Support Program (JSSP), which first began in mid-2005. The main focus of JSSP is to build the capacity of Afghanistan's criminal justice system through training and

---

[70] An OIG report from February 2010 stated: "Without INL's financial resources, the Embassy's ROL and justice programs would be seriously weakened. INL funds the Embassy's efforts to build a sustainable nationwide criminal justice system and a Justice Sector Support Program that runs a capacity building and mentoring program with a staff of over 100 U.S. and Afghan legal and support personnel." U.S. Department of State and Broadcasting Board of Governors, OIG, Report No. ISP-I-06-13A, February 2010, p. 39.

mentoring of justice sector personnel, including prosecution and defense services, the Attorney General's Office (AGO) and the Ministry of Justice (MOJ). Other areas of support include access to justice, gender justice issues, anti-corruption, legislative drafting, legal education and training, and public legal services.

JSSP funds 32 U.S. justice sector advisors and 45 Afghan legal consultants who have experience and expertise as prosecutors, judges, defense attorneys, and other criminal justice system professionals, as well as additional support personnel.[71] Through JSSP programming, more than 2,000 justice professionals, including judges, prosecutors, criminal investigative police, defense attorneys, victim and gender justice advocates, and others from 30 of 34 provinces have been trained since 2005. JSSP advisor teams are located in Kabul as well as in Herat, Balkh, Kunduz, Nangarhar, and Paktiya. INL plans on placing additional JSSP advisor teams in Kandahar and Bamyan as well potentially doubling the number of U.S. justice sector advisors and Afghan legal consultants involved in JSSP programs.

In Kabul, the primary target Afghan agencies of JSSP programs include the AGO and MOJ. The JSSP program provides support to the AGO through training and mentoring, as well as advising the Afghan Attorney General on various issues, including anti-corruption enforcement, police-prosecutor coordination, gender issues, administrative reform, and legal reform. JSSP provides support to the MOJ and its key directorates, including the Policy and Strategy Unit, which provides policy and organizational reform advice to the Justice Minister.

Other JSSP-funded support includes the development of a curriculum for the training of future Afghan prosecutors in the *Stage* course, which is a 12-month professional legal training program that follows undergraduate courses in law. The curriculum in development addresses issues such as gender justice and anti-corruption. Other projects to support access to justice include mentoring and capacity building for defense attorneys and private legal defense organizations.[72] Advisors outside of Kabul focus on police-prosecutor training and promote access to justice by holding provincial justice conferences and training defense attorneys. Additionally, JSSP provides support to the Anti-Corruption Unit (ACU).

Corrections System Support Program (CSSP)

The Corrections System Support Program (CSSP), managed by the State Department's INL Bureau, is the primary civilian-led corrections assistance program provided by the U.S. government to Afghanistan. U.S. corrections assistance began in 2005 as part of JSSP, and was subsequently split off in 2006 as a stand-alone program. CSSP was created in response to lagging international attention to the Afghan corrections system as the prisoner population grew from approximately 400 to 600 prisoners in the early 2000s to roughly 16,000 today.[73] From 2007 to

---

[71] U.S. Department of State, INL Bureau, "Rule of Law Programs: Afghanistan," Fact Sheet, May 3, 2010. Implementers of JSSP efforts vary, including private contractors and other parts of the U.S. government, such as the U.S. Departments of Justice and the Treasury.

[72] U.S. Department of State and Broadcasting Board of Governors, OIG, Report No. ISP-I-08-09, January 2008, p. 34.

[73] U.S. Department of State response to CRS request, June 17, 2010. The corrections officer training programs implemented by INL's CSSP seeks to improve conditions in prisons to which the program has access. Other donor nations are also involved in corrections support including Canada (in Kandahar), the United Kingdom (training in key provinces—e.g., Kandahar, Helmand, and Lashkar Gah); Italy (a women's prison in Herat); the Netherlands, and UNAMA.

2008 alone Afghanistan's prison population reportedly grew 21%.[74] As with other aspects of the Afghan justice system, a State Department Inspector General (OIG) report on ROL efforts in Afghanistan describes Afghan corrections as suffering from poorly trained staff, inadequate pay, crumbling buildings, and poor connections to the other components of the justice sector.[75]

CSSP's goal is to train, mentor, and advise the Ministry of Justice's Central Prison Directorate (CPD) in developing a safe and humane prison system that will not radicalize prisoners.[76] Space for the growing number of prisoners and the quality of existing facilities are priorities for support to the Afghan corrections system.[77] Among its major projects, CSSP provides capacity building and infrastructure support to the corrections system. One example of a capacity building project is the development of a prisoner tracking system that will track both pretrial and sentenced prisoners. The system is intended to allow defendants to be tracked as they enter and move through various stages of the justice system process. It also helps to prevent prisoners from being held for longer periods than is legally permitted or required.[78]

Infrastructure support to the Afghan corrections system through CSSP includes the construction of new facilities and rehabilitation of existing ones. For example, CSSP is supporting the renovation and reconstruction of the Pol-i-Charkhi Prison, which includes related training, staffing and equipping. In addition, CSSP funding also supports operations and maintenance costs for the Counternarcotics Justice Center (CNJC) in Kabul, a secure facility built by the Army Corps of Engineers that houses the Counternarcotics Criminal Justice Task Force (CJTF), the Central Narcotics Tribunal (CNT), and a detention center.[79]

Other CSSP assistance projects also include support for pay and rank reform for corrections officers; programs to address the special needs of vulnerable prisoner populations, including women and juveniles; and the development of prisoner vocational industries, such as carpet weaving, to support prisoner reintegration and reeducation.[80] In collaboration with the Combined Joint Interagency Task Force 435 (CJIATF-435), CSSP is establishing a new mobile team to assess prisons.[81] CSSP projects are implemented through approximately 60 corrections advisors.

As part of CSSP's training mission, more than 3,800 Afghan corrections staff have received training. Courses have included basic training and several advance and specialized courses, such as emergency response team training, English language programs, and special training for dealing

---

[74] DOD, Report on Progress Toward Security, June 2009, p. 46.

[75] U.S. Department of State and Broadcasting Board of Governors, OIG, Report No. ISP-I-08-09, January 2008, pp. 35-36.

[76] Ibid, p. 39.

[77] Although there are provincial-level corrections facilities in all 34 provinces of Afghanistan, according to the 2008 State Department OIG report, half of these facilities are rented, many of them residential houses converted into prisons. The situation is reportedly worse among the 203 district-level detention centers. U.S. Department of State and Broadcasting Board of Governors, OIG, Report No. ISP-I-06-13A, February 2010, pp. 35-36.

[78] According to experts, such a program was considered essential for ensuring that prisoners were not being illegally detained, reducing the size of inmate populations, and reducing the opportunity for corruption by CPD staff, prosecutors, and judges. See. U.S. Department of State and Broadcasting Board of Governors, OIG, Report No. ISP-I-08-9, January 2008, p. 41.

[79] DOD, Report on Progress Toward Security, June 2008, p. 35.

[80] DOD, Report on Progress Toward Security, June 2009, p. 546; and U.S. Department of State response to CRS request, June 17, 2010.

[81] U.S. Department of State response to CRS request, June 17, 2010.

with female inmates. Trainings are mainly conducted at training centers located in Kabul (at the Central Training Center) and at the Regional Training Centers (RTCs).[82] Completion of the basic training curriculum is a prerequisite for a corrections officer to be included in any pay reform or salary supplement support program.[83]

ROL Stabilization (RLS) Program

The ROL Stabilization (RLS) program is USAID's follow-on to the Afghanistan ROL Project (ARoLP), which began in October 2004 and ended in June 2009. After roughly a year's hiatus due in part to contracting issues, the RLS program began in mid-2010. There are two parts to USAID's program, implemented in Afghanistan through two separate private contractors. One component focuses on the formal justice sector, primarily the courts system. A second component focuses on the informal justice sector.

The formal component of the RLS program expands upon prior efforts under ARoLP to work with the Ministry of Justice, the Supreme Court, and the faculties of law and *Sharia* at private and public universities. Such efforts are intended to improve the capacity of the formal court system and raise citizens' awareness of their legal rights and how the judicial system operates. Originally introduced under ARoLP, the current RLS program will continue the release and implementation of an Afghanistan Case Assignment System (ACAS) in all Afghan courts. ACAS is designed to track and assign cases to judges across the judicial system. It is intended to strengthen the capacity of the Supreme Court to monitor and discipline judges, collect statistics on case flow, and make them publically available.

The formal component of the RLS program also expands upon prior efforts to emphasize training and vetting of judges for corruption cases, particularly those involved in the recently established Anti-Corruption Tribunal (ACT). Planned efforts to support court capacity building under the formal component program include judicial administrative reform for pay and grade levels, infrastructure and financial management assistance, as well as judicial training at the national, provincial, and district levels.[84] Under the formal component, the academic faculties of law and *Sharia* also receive support for legal study tours for Afghan law professors and curriculum development for the Supreme Court's judicial candidate training program (the judicial *stage*).

The informal component of the RLS program is a new element to USAID's ROL programming in Afghanistan.[85] It is intended to be a one-year pilot program, beginning mid-2010, to provide immediate access to justice through shuras in cleared and held districts. The four pilot districts or villages include two in Kandahar Province (Arghandab and Dand) and two in Nangarhar Province (Besood and Sikh Rod). Planned activities include establishing links between the informal and formal justice sectors, including providing transportation to justice sector facilities and facilitating case referrals between the two systems; mapping the operation and function of the informal

---

[82] These courses are based on international and U.N. human rights standards and developed in conjunction with the Afghan government. Through CSSP, leadership-level corrections officers have also been taken on a study tour of corrections facilities in the United States.

[83] U.S. Department of State and Broadcasting Board of Governors, OIG, Report No. ISP-I-08-09, January 2008, pp. 35-36.

[84] USAID response to CRS requests, June 2010.

[85] Ibid.

justice system; funding quick-impact projects, such as refurbishing justice facilities; and training and mentoring tribal elders and religious leaders.

Senior Federal Prosecutors Program

With funds from the State Department's INL Bureau, DOJ maintains a program to send DOJ prosecutors to Afghanistan to provide legal mentoring and training to build investigatory and prosecutorial capacity to combat corruption, drug trafficking, and other serious crimes. DOJ's focus has been to provide legal training and assistance to the Afghan Criminal Justice Task Force (CJTF), a specialized law enforcement entity for narcotics cases, and the Afghan Major Crimes Task Force (MCTF), a specialized crime investigation unit designed to address the most serious cases of corruption, kidnapping, and organized crime. Additionally DOJ supports the Attorney General Office's anti-corruption unit (ACU), and also provides other training initiatives for provincial judges, prosecutors, and investigators at Provincial Reconstruction Team (PRT) and Regional Training Center (RTC) locations outside of Kabul. Participating DOJ attorneys have also assisted Afghan officials with drafting several key legal documents, including a comprehensive counternarcotics law, military courts legislation and military courts penal and procedural law, as well as counterterrorism and extradition laws. The Senior Federal Prosecutors Program also provides criminal law advice to the U.S. Embassy in Afghanistan, Afghan government leadership, and U.S. law enforcement, as needed.

As of October 2010, there are eight DOJ attorneys based in Kabul participating in the Senior Federal Prosecutors Program.[86] They were recruited from the 93 U.S. Attorney's Offices in the United States for a tour in Afghanistan that lasts between one year and one-and-a-half years. Current DOJ plans are to expand the program from seven U.S. federal prosecutors to 15 by the end of 2010 and 21 by the end of 2011. In collaboration with the DOJ attorneys, the FBI also provides criminal investigatory training and mentoring initiatives to the same Afghan entities.

Defense Department Initiatives

As part of its counterinsurgency (COIN) and stability operations, and in conjunction with its civilian counterparts, the U.S. military provides various support to the justice sector in Afghanistan, particularly at the provincial and district levels. DOD support is provided through its PRTs, District Support Teams (DSTs), a division-level ROL team, and brigade-level Judge Advocate Generals. Since 2008, the U.S. military has held Key Leader Engagement meetings (KLEs) with provincial-level chief justices and other justice sector officials to facilitate cooperation with local officials on the development of justice sector infrastructure, training, and security of judges and courts.[87] With funds from the Commander's Emergency Response Program (CERP), the U.S. military provides infrastructure support to improve provincial and district level judicial systems, including building or rehabilitating and furnishing prisons, detention facilities, and courthouses.

DOD's CJTF-101, which operates within ISAF Regional Command-E (RC-E), supports judicial and prosecutor training. Training efforts have included the Continuing Legal Education program. Through its Provincial Reconstruction Teams (PRTs), the U.S. military has offered quarterly

---

[86] U.S. Department of Justice response to CRS request, May 2010.

[87] DOD, *Rule of Law Handbook*, 3rd ed., p. 289.

Continuing Legal Education programs on varying legal topics, including commercial law, criminal law, land disputes, civil rights, and gender justice to local judges, attorneys, prosecutors, corrections officers, and police officials.[88] Under another justice sector initiative, called the "mobile courts/circuit rider initiative," DOD utilizes assets to enable secure transport of judges and prosecutors into non-permissive areas. At the national level, the U.S. military is also involved in police-justice sector integration through support to the Afghan Ministry of Interior's Legal Advisor's Office. Through its Provincial Reconstruction Teams (PRTs), the military also helps to produce and distribute legal texts and legal awareness materials for the radio and in print.

The Defense Department is also increasingly supporting the training and mentoring of Afghan corrections and other aspects of the Afghan justice sector through Combined Joint Interagency Task Force 435 (CJIATF-435) and ongoing efforts to transition detention operations in Afghanistan to the Afghan government. CJIATF-435 is a July 2010 follow-on to Joint Task Force 435 (JTF-435), which was established in September 2009 and became operational in January 2010. JTF-435 assumed responsibility for U.S. detention operations in Parwan, including oversight of the detainee review processes, programs to facilitate the reintegration of detainees into society, and support for the promotion of the ROL in Afghanistan through corrections-related training and mentoring.[89] As JTF-435 evolved into CJIATF-435, it has become engaged in a broader range of ROL support activities, including developing Afghan investigative, prosecutorial, and judicial capabilities.[90]

Selected Other Justice Sector Programs

Several additional ROL assistance programs implemented by other agencies also are funded mainly by the State Department, though they are smaller in funding and scope of purpose. They include support for the following:

- **Major Crimes Task Force (MCTF).** With funding mainly from the Defense Department, the FBI provides support to the Major Crimes Task Force (MCTF), an Afghan interagency entity designed to investigate high-level crimes related to public corruption and organized crime.

- **Sensitive Investigations Unit (SIU).** With funding from the Defense Department and the State Department, DEA supports the Afghan Sensitive Investigations Unit (SIU). While the Sensitive Investigations Unit's primary purpose is the investigation of high-level drug-related criminal cases, investigations may also involve high-level corruption cases.

- **Judicial Security.** The U.S. Marshals Service (USMS) provides judicial security assistance to the Ministry of Interior's security personnel assigned to the Counternarcotics Judicial Center (CNJC). Several members of the Marshals' Tactical Operations Division Special Operations Group are in Kabul.

---

[88] Ibid, p. 267.

[89] See for example U.S. Central Command (CENTCOM), "Afghan Ministers Accept Responsibility of Parwan Detention Facility," available at http://www.centcom.mil/news/afghan-ministers-accept-responsibility-of-parwan-detention-facility.

[90] DOD, Report on Progress Toward Security and Stability in Afghanistan and United States Plan for Sustaining the Afghan National Security Forces, April 2010, p. 54.

- **High Office of Oversight (HOO).** Between FY2011 and FY2013, USAID plans to provide the High Office of Oversight (HOO) $30 million to build capacity at the central and provincial level, according to USAID officials. By the end of the first quarter of 2010, USAID will have reportedly provided $1.4 million in start-up assistance to the HOO.[91] USAID would pay for salaries of six High Office of Oversight senior staff and provides some information technology systems as well. Plans also include support for HOO to decentralize in conjunction with the establishment of regional Anti Corruption Tribunals.

- **Legal Education.** With grant funding from the State Department's INL Bureau, the University of Washington brings Afghan law professors to the United States, where they can enroll in law school courses and obtain certificates or Master of Law (LLM) degrees. Also with grant funding from the State Department's INL Bureau, the International Association of Women Judges (IAWJ) provides support to Afghan women in the legal profession.

- **Research on the Informal Justice Sector.** With funding from the State Department's INL Bureau, the U.S. Institute of Peace (USIP) has conducted, since mid-2007, studies on linkages between the formal and informal justice systems in Afghanistan. As part of the project, USIP conducted studies on the informal justice sector in four pilot districts that span both rural and urban environments—two districts in Herat, one district in Nangahar, and one district in Paktya.

- **Multilateral Trust Funds.** With funding from the State Department's INL Bureau, the U.S. government contributes to multilateral funds that address salary reform for judges, prosecutors, and corrections personnel.

Selected Crosscutting ROL Programs

In addition to assistance programs specifically to the justice sector, discussed above, other crosscutting efforts have an impact on ROL goals. These include programs to strengthen the capacity of general Afghan governance, anti-corruption, women's issues, counternarcotics, and the Afghan security forces, particularly the Afghan National Police.

Anti-corruption

As discussed above, widespread practices of corruption are generally attributed as undermining international efforts to establish ROL in Afghanistan. U.S. efforts to combat Afghan corruption overlap with U.S. efforts to strengthen the justice sector, particularly regarding support to investigate, prosecute, and incarcerate corrupt actors. In addition to such programs, the U.S. government is involved in other anti-corruption efforts, beyond the scope of Afghan justice sector assistance, but with theoretically positive consequences for strengthening ROL in Afghanistan. For example, NATO commander Gen. Petraeus established in mid-2010 an anti-corruption task force to address and prevent future allegations of defense contractor funds from being siphoned off by corrupt businesses, warlords, or insurgents.[92] A U.S. interagency effort established last year

---

[91] USAID response to CRS, January 2010.

[92] Maria Abi-Habib and Matthew Rosenberg, "Task Force to Take on Afghan Corruption," *Wall Street Journal*, June 18, 2010. News sources indicates that part of the impetus for establishing this task force was to address concerns (continued...)

---

to track and disrupt Taliban finances is reportedly increasingly focused on tracking corruption-related finances.[93] Other U.S.-issued anti-corruption directives delineate procedures regarding how U.S. officials in Afghanistan should proceed when they identify incidents of corruption occurring.

Other examples include USAID's commercial law and trade facilitation support programs.[94] USAID's Economic Growth and Governance Initiative (EGGI) is designed to advance the anticorruption agenda by streamlining business registration and licensing procedures; improving mining, telecommunications, insurance, and energy regulation; strengthening supervision of the banking sector and improved financial intermediation; and enhanced reporting and collection of tax and non-tax revenues into the Central Treasury. USAID's Trade Access and Facilitation in Afghanistan (TAFA) project supports efforts to streamline and simplify the customs clearance process. The goal of such efforts is to reducing time and payments for trading across borders, which otherwise provide opportunities for corruption.

Civil Service Capacity Building

A central limiting factor to efforts to strengthen ROL and the capacity of the justice sector is the overall weakness of Afghanistan's civil service capacity to manage the day-to-day operations of a modern bureaucracy. According to several DOD reports to Congress, the Afghan government is fundamentally limited by a lack of civil service capacity, human capacity, resources, and interagency planning and coordination.[95] The absence of sufficient amounts of educated human capital to draw from particularly hampers Afghan ministry efforts to implement programs and deliver public services at all levels.[96] To address this, USAID administers the Afghanistan Civil Service Support (ACSS) program, previously the Capacity Development Program, which supports efforts to train civil servants throughout Afghanistan in public administration. In 2010, more than 15,000 training sessions have been planned to support civil service development at the national and sub-national levels in five common administrative functions: financial management, project management, human resources management, procurement, and policy and strategic planning.[97]

Local Governance Support

Analysts widely agree that Afghan government capacity and performance has generally been more effective at the national level in Kabul than out at the provincial and district levels.[98] To

---

(...continued)

discussed in a June 2010 report by the majority staff of the House Committee on Oversight and Government Reform, Subcommittee on National Security and Foreign Affairs, entitled *Warlord, Inc.: Extortion and Corruption Along the U.S. Supply Chain in Afghanistan*.

[93] Abi-Habib and Rosenberg.

[94] USAID response to CRS, January 2010.

[95] DOD, Report on Progress Toward Security, January 2009, pp. 7-8. See also CRS Report RS21922, *Afghanistan: Politics, Elections, and Government Performance*, by Kenneth Katzman, and CRS Report RL30588, *Afghanistan: Post-Taliban Governance, Security, and U.S. Policy*, by Kenneth Katzman.

[96] Ibid, p. 10.

[97] DOD, Report on Progress Toward Security and Stability in Afghanistan and United States Plan for Sustaining the Afghan National Security Forces, April 2010, pp. 49-50.

[98] DOD, Report on Progress Toward Security, January 2009, p. 50; U.S. Department of State and Broadcasting Board (continued...)

---

address this general tendency for Afghan government policy planning and functions to be less effective at local levels, USAID administers the Local Governance and Community Development program (LGCD) and the Afghan Municipal Strengthening Program to provide provincial and district governance capacity building, as well as an expanded focus on major urban municipalities. Though the scope of the Local Governance and Community Development program is broader than support specifically to the Afghan justice sector, it indirectly seeks to facilitate the expansion of ROL governance principles to the provincial and district levels.

Anti-money Laundering

Vulnerabilities in Afghanistan's financial regulatory system have raised concerns about the likelihood that potentially significant sums of money may be laundered or otherwise illegally moved through the Afghan financial channels.[99] Such vulnerabilities may include not only the formal banking system, but also bulk cash smuggling and informal value transfer mechanisms, such as *hawala*. The Department of the Treasury administers technical assistance to the Financial Intelligence Unit (FIU) at Afghanistan's central bank, which has covered financial sector oversight, supervision and enforcement as well as guidance in the registration of money service businesses.[100] Other U.S. government agencies are also involved in various other efforts to track and investigate potential Afghan financial crimes.

Land Reform

Land and property disputes represent the largest proportion of civil law cases in Afghanistan. To address this, USAID administers the Land Reform in Afghanistan project, valued at up to $140 million over five years beginning in FY2010. This project is intended to support efforts to reduce corruption in land transactions by raising awareness among citizens about land processes and procedures, by reducing the number of steps and preventing delays in land transactions, and by establishing a legal and regulatory framework to standardize land administration and property disputes.[101]

Parliamentary Support

To improve institutional checks and balances through the legislative branch, USAID supports various programs to assist the Afghan National Assembly.[102] Under one program, the Afghanistan Parliamentary Assistance Program (APAP), USAID supports the Budget Committee's capacity to understand, analyze, and oversee the budgeting process. Another program assists the Afghan Parliament's National Economic Commission to understand and support adoption of modern

---

(...continued)

of Governors, OIG, Report No. ISP-I-08-09, January 2008, pp. 19-20. See also CRS Report RS21922, *Afghanistan: Politics, Elections, and Government Performance*, by Kenneth Katzman, and CRS Report RL30588, *Afghanistan: Post-Taliban Governance, Security, and U.S. Policy*, by Kenneth Katzman.

[99] Matthew Rosenberg, "Corruption Suspected in Airlift of Billions in Cash from Kabul," *Wall Street Journal*, June 26, 2010.

[100] DOD, Report on Progress Toward Security, January 2009, p. 52.

[101] DOD, Report on Progress Toward Security and Stability in Afghanistan and United States Plan for Sustaining the Afghan National Security Forces, April 2010, p. 68.

[102] USAID response to CRS, January 2010.

economic, commercial and financial legislation, and efforts to conduct cost-benefit analysis as a tool for economic decision-making.

Women's Issues

In addition to the gender justice component of the JSSP, the State Department provides additional support to women's issues through the Increasing Women's Rights and Access to Justice in Afghanistan Program and the Advancing Human Rights and Women's Rights within an Islamic Framework Program. Such programs are intended to train and educate male and female police officers, prosecutors, defense attorneys, corrections officers, and others in civil society on gender-sensitive interpretations and applications of the penal code sections that affect women.[103]

Trafficking in Persons

The State Department funds efforts to build the capacity of the Afghan government to investigate and prosecute human trafficking cases, as well as to provide training to improve victim identification, referral mechanisms, and the management and reporting of trafficking cases. Target government officials include police officers, judges, and prosecutors.[104]

Counternarcotics

Law enforcement and justice sector reform represents one of the five key pillars in the U.S. government's counternarcotics strategy for Afghanistan. To support this goal, the State Department, DOJ, particularly DEA, and DOD maintain several programs that are intended to enhance the Afghan judicial system as it relates to counternarcotics, train prosecutors, and build the infrastructure necessary to indict, arrest, try, convict, and incarcerate drug traffickers.[105]

The State Department, for example, provides funding to DOJ for the mentoring of Afghan investigators and prosecutors on the Criminal Justice Task Force and Afghan judges on the Central Narcotics Tribunal, both of which are co-located at the Counternarcotics Justice Center (CNJC), as well as the Provincial Counternarcotics Training Program. With State Department and DOD funding, DEA supports, trains, and equips specialized counternarcotics law enforcement units within the Afghan Counternarcotics Police (CNP), including the National Interdiction Unit (NIU), the Sensitive Investigative Unit (SIU), and the Technical Investigative Unit. These Afghan officers work with the DEA Kabul Country Office and the DEA Foreign-deployed Advisory Support Teams (FAST) on investigations. DOD also provides military support to Afghan counternarcotics forces through the Combined Joint Interagency Task Force–Nexus (CJIATF-N) and through the DOD-supported Afghan Counternarcotics Training Academy.

---

[103] Ibid, p. 72.

[104] U.S. Department of State, INL Bureau, Program and Budget Guide, FY2010.

[105] DOJ's ICITAP is also assisting the Department of Defense in their efforts to build the organizational capacity of the Afghan counternarcotics police.

Police Assistance

Building and reforming the ANP is primarily a security mission in Afghanistan, but with significant implications for ROL. With DOD funding and State Department program support, Afghan National Police are trained, equipped, and mentored through the Focused District Development (FDD) program and other targeted efforts for the Criminal Investigations Division, Counternarcotics Police, Counterterrorism Police, Afghan National Civil Order Police, Kabul City Police, Afghan Provincial Police, and Afghan Border Police.

Conclusion: Outlook on Issues in the 112th Congress

Current Administration policy emphasizes expanding and improving Afghan governance as a long-term means of stabilizing Afghanistan, in recognition of the essential role effective ROL plays in securing Afghanistan. Yet, the weak performance of and lack of transparency within the Afghan government are growing factors in debate over the effectiveness of U.S. strategy in Afghanistan. Congress has been active in all aspects of U.S. policy toward Afghanistan, including authorizing and appropriating ROL-related programs and assistance, as well as conducting oversight on policy implementation and effectiveness.

In the context of broader congressional interest in the evaluation, oversight, and funding of the overall U.S. effort in Afghanistan, the following sections identify several issues for Congress related to U.S. efforts to strengthen ROL and the justice sector in Afghanistan. These include recent Afghan corruption allegations and implications for congressional funding, criticism of ROL support efforts by program evaluators, U.S. support to the informal justice sector, and the future of U.S. support to Afghan ROL.

Corruption Allegations and Implications for Congressional Funding

Heightened alarm over the extent and scale of corruption in Afghanistan has spurred policymakers to question the direction of U.S. policy in Afghanistan under the Obama Administration. U.S. assistance to Afghanistan for FY2011 is under particular congressional scrutiny due to press allegations in June 2010 that corrupt Afghan officials may be pocketing billions of U.S. aid and logistics funding and siphoning it out of Afghanistan's Kabul Airport to financial safe havens elsewhere.[106] Major concerns for Congress are whether U.S. assistance to Afghanistan is susceptible to waste, fraud, and diversion; whether such aid funds may be in part fueling Afghan corruption; and what can the U.S. government do to address potential vulnerabilities.

In June 2010, Representative Nita Lowey, Chair of the House Appropriations Subcommittee responsible for the State Department's Foreign Operations budget, announced that she would place a hold on certain U.S. aid to Afghanistan until she has "confidence that U.S. taxpayer money is not being abused to line the pockets of corrupt Afghan government officials, drug lords,

---

[106] Matthew Rosenberg, "Corruption Suspected in Airlift of Billions in Cash from Kabul," *Wall Street Journal*, June 26, 2010.

and terrorists."[107] Following such allegations and congressional concern, several congressional hearings in July 2010 on the issue of civilian assistance to Afghanistan ensued. While the specific allegations of corruption were not confirmed, witnesses generally acknowledged corruption in Afghanistan to be a major impediment to establishing effective ROL efforts and overall reconstruction goals.[108] Earlier in 2009, Representative Dave Obey, Chair of the House Appropriations Committee, also emphasized concerns regarding corruption and the need for specific and measurable benchmarks for anti-corruption improvement to justify future U.S. commitments Afghanistan.[109]

Recent concerns over corruption have also prompted a broader policy debate over the relative importance of fighting corruption among other U.S. strategic priorities in Afghanistan. Central questions in current debates include the following:

- How far should the U.S. government go in combating corruption in Afghanistan?

- Are there limits in the extent to which anti-corruption should be a priority in U.S. strategy to Afghanistan?

- How should anti-corruption investigations in Afghanistan be conducted and resolved? Through due process of Afghan law? Through diplomatic negotiation? Or with or without overt endorsement from President Karzai and other top-level Afghan officials?

On the one hand, Obama Administration policy, as articulated in two major Afghanistan policy addresses on March 27, 2009, and December 1, 2009, emphasizes the need for more to be done to combat corruption within the Afghan government. The latter Obama statement, for example, specified that "the days of providing a blank check are over" for the Afghan government if it does

---

[107] Greg Miller, "U.S. Lawmaker to Withhold $3.9 Billion in Afghan Aid over Corruption Problems," *Washington Post*, June 29, 2010. On September 30, 2010, Congress enacted P.L. 111-242, making continuing appropriations from FY2010 through December 3, 2010. However, P.L. 111-242 does not make reference to changes in the level of U.S. aid to Afghanistan.

[108] See for example hearings on July 15, 2010, and July 28, 2010, held by the House Appropriations Committee, Subcommittee on State, Foreign Operations, and Related Programs, on Civilian Assistance for Afghanistan. These recent hearings follow on long-standing congressional interest on aspects of U.S. ROL-related efforts in Afghanistan, ranging from security assistance coordination, progress in training and equipping the Afghan National Police, and counternarcotics efforts. See for example the July 21, 2010, hearing on "International Counternarcotics Policies" held by the House Oversight and Government Reform Committee, Subcommittee on Domestic Policy; the April 15, 2010 hearing on "Contracts for Afghan National Police Training" held by the Senate Homeland Security and Governmental Affairs Committee, Subcommittee on Contracting Oversight; the April 14, 2010, hearing on "President Obama's Fiscal 2011 Budget Request for the State Department's Security Assistance" held by House Appropriations Committee, Subcommittee on State, Foreign Operations, and Related Programs; the February 22, 2010, hearing on "Coordination Efforts in Iraq and Afghanistan" held by the Commission on Wartime Contracting; the December 18, 2009, hearing on "Contractor Training of the Afghan National Security Force" held by the Commission on Wartime Contracting; the March 26, 2009, hearing on "Troops, Diplomats and Aid: Assessing Strategic Resources for Afghanistan" held by the House Oversight and Government Reform, Subcommittee on National Security and Foreign Affairs; and the February 12, 2009, hearing on "Training and Equipping Afghan Security Forces: Unaccounted Weapons and Strategic Challenges" held by the House Oversight and Government Reform, Subcommittee on National Security and Foreign Affairs. Additionally, the House Committee on Oversight and Government Reform, Subcommittee on National Security and Foreign Affairs, held a hearing on ROL programs in Afghanistan in June 2008. See U.S. House of Representatives, Committee on Oversight and Government Reform, Subcommittee on National Security and Foreign Affairs, Hearing on "Oversight of U.S. Efforts to Train and Equip Police and Enhance the Justice Sector in Afghanistan," June 18, 2008.

[109] See for example House Committee on Appropriations, Statement by Rep. Dave Obey, "Obey Statement: 2009 Supplemental Appropriations for Iraq, Afghanistan, Pakistan, and Pandemic Flu," May 4, 2009.

not reduce corruption and deliver services. Supporters of such a policy approach have emphasized the importance of anti-corruption efforts in an overall counterinsurgency (COIN) strategy in Afghanistan, focused on improving Afghan perceptions of the Afghan government's legitimacy and transparency. Supporters would also emphasize the importance of anti-corruption efforts in plugging some of the most serious corruption-related leaks, including, potentially, the recently reported bulk cash movements out of the Kabul Airport. Recent Afghan investigations involving several U.S.-supported anti-corruption and oversight agencies may also be indicative of improvements in Afghan government capacity to combat corruption.

Others, however, have questioned whether the benefits of anti-corruption efforts in Afghanistan outweigh several drawbacks. For example, recent high-profile corruption investigations targeting prominent Karzai supports have had the unintended consequence of aggravating U.S.-Karzai relations and also potentially undermining recent U.S. successes in strengthening Afghan anti-corruption capabilities.[110] Some observers have discussed the possible need to avoid investigating and prosecuting particular high-level Afghan officials to avoid future complications in the U.S. government's relationship with President Karzai.[111] Observers suggest that such an approach, while potentially beneficial from a diplomatic perspective, may risk facilitating the existing perceptions among many Afghans that high-level corrupt officials are exempt from the full force of Afghan law. Other observers have also argued that meaningful improvements in combating corruption in Afghanistan require a long-term U.S. commitment to stay in Afghanistan for potentially decades. Short of that, such observers predict that prioritizing anti-corruption will yield limited success.[112]

Criticisms of ROL Support Efforts by Program Evaluators

As Congress conducts oversight and appropriates funding for U.S. assistance programs to support ROL in Afghanistan, an issue to consider is the extent to which the Afghan government can absorb and effectively use such assistance. Such sentiments have been variously confirmed by the Special Inspector General for Afghanistan Reconstruction (SIGAR), U.S. Government Accountability Office (GAO), the State Department's Office of the Inspector General (OIG), and others in legislatively mandated reports to Congress on the status of U.S. ROL efforts in Afghanistan.[113] Collectively, these reports indicate that although significant progress in establishing ROL in Afghanistan have been achieved, there appear to be several fundamental limitations on the ability of the U.S. government and other donors to strengthen the Afghan justice sector in the short term.

---

[110] See for example Greg Miller, "U.S. Anti-Graft Effort," *Washington Post*, September 13, 2010.

[111] See for example Rajiv Chandrasekaran, "A Subtler Tack," *Washington Post*, September 13, 2010.

[112] See for example Mark Mazzetti, "As Time Passes, the Goals Shrink," *New York Times*, September 12, 2010. One interviewee stated: "We've sort of backed ourselves into a corner by putting effective governance at the forefront. Unless you are prepared to stay in Afghanistan with high troop levels for at least a decade, then an overt campaign to tackle corruption is a big mistake."

[113] Recent examples include SIGAR, "U.S. Reconstruction Efforts in Afghanistan Would Benefit from a Finalized Comprehensive U.S. Anti-Corruption Strategy," Report No. 10-15, August 5, 2010; SIGAR, Report No. 10-2, December 16, 2009; SIGAR, Report No. 10-8, April 4, 2010; U.S. Department of State and Broadcasting Board of Governors, OIG, Report No. ISP-I-06-13A, February 2010; U.S. Department of State and Broadcasting Board of Governors, OIG, Report No. ISP-I-08-09, January 2008; GAO, Report No. GAO-09-473SP, April 2009. Ongoing SIGAR work related to ROL in Afghanistan include audits on U.S. and international efforts to build Afghanistan's capacity, including at the provincial level, to combat corruption, review of the U.S. civilian uplift in Afghanistan, and salary supplements provided to Afghan government officials with USAID funding.

For example, a 2009 GAO report identified low literacy rates and the related lack of basic computer skills as fundamental limiting factors for the recruitment of Afghan justice sector personnel, including police, prosecutors, investigators, and administrative staff, as well as for the ability to implement a modern management system for the justice sector.[114] Retention of trained staff is also challenging as many reportedly leave Afghan ministries for better paying jobs with donor countries and NGOs. Separately, a 2010 State Department OIG report warned that there is "tension" between, on the one hand, the U.S. government's stated goals for ROL in Afghanistan, and on the other hand, the capacity and commitment of the Afghan government to implement such ambitions.[115]

Also missing are components of an effective ROL and anti-corruption program, according to program evaluators. Additional reported concerns included the following:

- The lack of both a formally approved ROL strategy and an anti-corruption strategy for Afghanistan limits the U.S. Embassy in Kabul from setting ROL and anti-corruption priorities and timelines, as well as identifying the appropriate number of personnel and needed skill sets, according to the State Department's OIG and SIGAR.[116]

- The need for improved ROL coordination and guidance between the U.S. Embassy in Kabul and Provincial Reconstruction Teams (PRTs) in the field, as well as improved reporting on ROL-related activities from the field to the U.S. Embassy in Kabul, according to the State Department's OIG.[117]

- The inability of Afghan anti-corruption and oversight institutions, such as the Afghan High Office of Oversight (HOO) and the Afghan Control and Audit Office (CAO), to function effectively due to the lack of independence, a weak legal framework, and lack of commitment from donors, including from the U.S. government, according to SIGAR.[118]

U.S. Support to the Informal Justice Sector

Observers have described current U.S. efforts to support Afghan ROL development, including increased emphasis on the informal justice sector and other civilian and military efforts to improve access to justice at the provincial and district level, to be in many ways unique and untested, due the sheer scale of the programs involved, the low level of existing justice sector capacity, gaps in U.S. government understanding of existing dispute resolution mechanisms throughout the country, the absence of security in many parts of Afghanistan, and the existence of entrenched corruption at all levels of the Afghan bureaucracy. This means that, while many U.S.

---

[114] GAO, Report No. GAO-09-473SP, April 2009, p. 25.

[115] U.S. Department of State and Broadcasting Board of Governors, OIG, Report No. ISP-I-06-13A, February 2010, p. 3.

[116] Ibid, pp. 36-37; and SIGAR, Report No. 10-15, August 5, 2010.

[117] U.S. Department of State and Broadcasting Board of Governors, OIG, Report No. ISP-I-06-13A, February 2010, p. 36.

[118] SIGAR, Report No. 10-2, December 16, 2009; and SIGAR, Report No. 10-8, April 4, 2010.

projects may be assessed as helping to improve the Afghan justice system, other U.S. projects, at times, may be perceived as ineffective or even counterproductive.[119]

In this vein, human rights and development advocates have questioned the value of funding U.S. programs to support the informal justice sector in Afghanistan. One concern is how deeply the international community, including the United States, should be involved in trying to ensure that the informal justice sector provides equitable justice. Some see supporting the traditional justice sector as an expedient means of building ties to local community leaders—a process that can improve the prospects for the U.S. counterinsurgency (COIN) strategy. Others believe that supporting use of the traditional justice system could harm the longer term objective of building a democratic and progressive Afghanistan by preserving some of its undemocratic traditional elements. Still others believe that policies to address the sector might be viewed by Afghans as intrusive. There are also some international officials who feel that reforming or overseeing these mechanisms is beyond the scope of the international stabilization mission in Afghanistan.

This debate is an issue of concern for U.S. lawmakers, given the recent strategic focus on improving Afghan access to justice and increased attention and funding to strengthen and support the informal justice sector in Afghanistan. Various analysts continue to disagree regarding the value and efficacy of U.S. support to the informal justice sector, with some, on the one hand, arguing that such support is vital, particularly in the short term, to ensure that increasing numbers of Afghans have access to fair and timely dispute resolution mechanisms. Others, on the other hand, argue that, given finite amounts of resources available to strengthen the justice sector, all of such resources should be devoted to strengthening the quality and reach of the formal justice sector.

The Future of U.S. Support to Afghan ROL

U.S. efforts to support ROL and anti-corruption in Afghanistan have evolved and grown since 2001, beginning with support to the Afghan Interim Authority, ratification in 2004 of the Afghan Constitution, and continuing through 2010 as the Obama Administration has sought to strengthen and expand the reach of Afghan justice institutions throughout the country. Proponents of the current U.S. approach to ROL institutions in Afghanistan would argue that it is informed by prior challenges and policy criticism and reflects a strategic evolution in the level of U.S. commitment, resources, and policy approach to ROL-related efforts in Afghanistan.

Observers continue to debate, however, whether or to what extent these shifts in the level of U.S. commitment and resources for ROL efforts in Afghanistan will help the U.S. government reach its ultimate goal of developing a stable, capable, and legitimate Afghan government. At stake in such a debate is the long-term effectiveness and value of continued congressional funding and policy support for the Obama Administration's efforts to strengthen ROL in Afghanistan. Already, some U.S. government assessments raise concerns about the long-term effectiveness of current efforts.

---

[119] See for example, a USAID-funded project to distribute among Afghan children, kites to fly at a local festival with slogans supporting the ROL and gender equality. According to news reports, kites were taken away by local police to fly them themselves and several girls who wanted to fly the kites were threatened by the police, resulting in few female kite fliers. Rod Nordland, "Afghan Equality and Law, but With Strings Attached," September 24, 2010; "Politics Ensnare U.S.-backed Kite Runners," Checkpoint Kabul, a McClatchy news blog, October 15, 2010.

In 2008, the State Department's Office of the Inspector General (OIG) concluded that "the many U.S. efforts to support ROL in Afghanistan are laudable for their professionalism and tenacity, but it is often not clear how, even if, ROL efforts are being measured for success, and when the intense international attention wanes, whether these projects can be sustained."[120] Separately, a Defense Department report in 2010 warned that there has been "little enduring progress despite significant investment toward reform, infrastructure and training"[121] in the justice sector and that while Afghanistan has "achieved some progress on anti-corruption, in particular with regard to legal and institutional reforms, real change remains elusive and political will, in particular, remains doubtful."[122] Afghan officials have also raised similar concerns, arguing that despite increasing resources devoted to justice sector support, efforts have not yet translated into a functional formal justice system in Afghanistan.[123] The 112th Congress may choose to address these long term issues in the context of the Obama Administration's review of U.S. strategy to Afghanistan, expected to take place in mid-2011. Other potential decision points for Congress may center on FY2011 appropriations and congressional review of the Administration's FY2012 budget request.

Related CRS Products

For additional CRS products on Afghanistan governance, military, security, assistance, and contractor issues, see:

CRS Report RS21922, *Afghanistan: Politics, Elections, and Government Performance*, by Kenneth Katzman

CRS Report RL30588, *Afghanistan: Post-Taliban Governance, Security, and U.S. Policy*, by Kenneth Katzman

CRS Report R40156, *War in Afghanistan: Strategy, Military Operations, and Issues for Congress*, by Steve Bowman and Catherine Dale

CRS Report R40699, *Afghanistan: U.S. Foreign Assistance*, by Curt Tarnoff

CRS Report RL32686, *Afghanistan: Narcotics and U.S. Policy*, by Christopher M. Blanchard

CRS Report R40764, *Department of Defense Contractors in Iraq and Afghanistan: Background and Analysis*, by Moshe Schwartz

CRS Report R40747, *United Nations Assistance Mission in Afghanistan: Background and Policy Issues*, by Rhoda Margesson

---

[120] U.S. Department of State and Broadcasting Board of Governors, OIG, Report No. ISP-I-08-09, January 2008, p. 2.

[121] DOD, Report on Progress Toward Security and Stability in Afghanistan and United States Plan for Sustaining the Afghan National Security Forces, April 2010, p. 52.

[122] Ibid, pp. 46, 52.

[123] See for example Nader Nadery, a commissioner in the Afghan Independent Human Rights Commission, "Peace Needs to Get Serious About Justice," *Parliamentary Brief*, September 2010.

Author Contact Information

Liana Sun Wyler
Analyst in International Crime and Narcotics
lwyler@crs.loc.gov, 7-6177

Kenneth Katzman
Specialist in Middle Eastern Affairs
kkatzman@crs.loc.gov, 7-7612

www.ingramcontent.com/pod-product-compliance
Lightning Source LLC
Chambersburg PA
CBHW080616290526

45790CB00007B/2806